Stop

Yourself Sick

Stop Making Yourself Sick

HAROLD PAUL ADOLPH, M.D.
with Dave Bourne

While this book is designed for the reader's personal enjoyment and profit, it is also intended for group study. A Leader's Guide with Victor Multiuse Transparency Masters is available from your local bookstore or from the publisher.

VICTOR BOOKS a division of SP Publications, Inc.
WHEATON, ILLINOIS 60187

Offices also in
Whitby, Ontario, Canada
Amersham-on-the-Hill, Bucks, England

The names in this book were changed to insure patients' confidentiality.

Under no circumstances should the information in this book be interpreted as medical advice.

Unless otherwise noted, Scripture quotations are from the *Holy Bible, New International Version,* © 1973, 1978, 1984, International Bible Society. Used by permission of Zondervan Bible Publishers. Other Scripture quotations are from the *King James Version* (KJV); the New American Standard Bible (NASB), © the Lockman Foundation, 1960, 1962, 1963, 1968, 1971, 1972, 1973, 1975, 1977; and *The Living Bible* (TLB), © 1971, Tyndale House Publishers, Wheaton, IL 60189. Used by permission.

Recommended Dewey Decimal Classification: 248.4
Suggested Subject Heading: CHRISTIAN LIFE

Library of Congress Catalog Card Number: 85-62715
ISBN: 0-89693-325-3

Contents

To my dedicated and loyal wife, Bonnie Jo, who has accompanied me around the world in the ministry of both physical and spiritual healing, and who taught our two children, David and Carolyn Joy, while we worked in Ethiopia.

—HAROLD P. ADOLPH, M.D.

To Beth, whose love, help, and support were invaluable to the completion of this book.

—DAVE BOURNE

Chapter One
The Breath of Life

Of all the cults in the United States, which one group would you think is largest? The Hare Krishnas? The followers of the Rev. Sun Myung Moon? The Mormons? Each of these groups certainly would be in contention for the title—but none even come close to qualifying.

Perhaps a few clues would help. The most influential cult in this country has more than doubled its membership in the last two decades. In fact, according to a recent Gallup Poll, a full 59 percent of all American men and women claim to adhere to its vigorous, daily rituals.

Many members profess to have experienced life-changing results after submitting to the cult's disciplines. Says one devotee, "I can do anything now. I'm superhuman." Another reports that for him, being a member of the cult has made the difference between "being alive and being the living dead."

The "cult" to which I am referring is, of course, the cult of physical fitness.

Ever since the early 1960s, when John F. Kennedy provided this nation with an inspiring model of youthful fitness, Americans have pursued the improvement of their bodies with an almost religious intensity. Swimming, bicycling, and jogging lead the pack of preferred exercises, while "ultra" events—which test the body's limits of strength and endurance—increasingly are coming into fashion. In New York City in 1984, for example, thirty-two runners participated in a six-day ultra-running event, eating and drinking while they ran, stopping only long enough to sleep a few hours each night. The winner of this race endured for 635 miles in 90-degree heat, high humidity, and frequent rainstorms.

But just when America's twenty-year love affair with the joys of fitness was reaching its zenith, tragedy struck. Perhaps more than any other individual, Jim Fixx had introduced the average man to the benefits of regular exercise. His best-selling *The Complete Book of Running* (Random House) was considered the classic in its field, a virtual Bible to the millions of Americans who fervently embraced the cult of fitness' articles of faith.

Then, suddenly, Fixx was dead. Ironically, he died of a heart attack—while jogging. Almost overnight the cult was thrown into a state of panic. With one of its leaders gone, members nervously began to question their practices. *Could we have been wrong all along?* they wondered. *Is exercise just a faster way to kill ourselves? Are its benefits really overrated?*

Others, though, in a moment of insight, saw the bottom line: If physical exercise alone could not guarantee longevity, what could? What could produce a sense of wellness and wholeness in a person's life?

The Neglected Factor

For all their preoccupation with lifting weights, playing tennis, and bicycling into oblivion, the devotees of fitness failed to recognize one fundamental truth: to experience wholeness, man cannot concentrate solely on physical exercise. He also must develop his *spiritual* health.

The fact is, a direct relationship exists between our spiritual health and our physical well-being. After nearly twenty-five years as a practicing physician and surgeon, I've found that people who are experiencing fellowship with God—whose spiritual lives are grounded in Him—can enjoy a significantly improved degree of physical health.

This may seem a rather bold assertion. But it is not without support. In Exodus, for example, we find:

> If you listen carefully to the voice of the Lord your God and do what is right in His eyes, if you pay attention to His commands and keep all His decrees, I will not bring on you any of the diseases I brought on the Egyptians, for I am the Lord who heals you (Ex. 15:26).

I'm Glad You Asked That

At this point, I'm sure you have a number of questions. You may be wondering, for example, if I believe that all sickness is the result of spiritual rebellion. Or you might want to know, since a healthy spiritual life is key to a healthy physical life, why so many dedicated Christians are suffering from painful or debilitating diseases.

These questions clearly deserve our attention.

Is all sickness the result of spiritual rebellion? If you took this book's premise and ran with it to an extreme, you *could* conclude that illness touches only those persons who disobey the Lord.

I once spoke with a doctor from Czechoslovakia who told me the story of three Communist physicians in his homeland who falsely accused him of malpractice. These doctors deliberately perjured themselves to frame the doctor and show their contempt for him. However, after testifying against their colleague, each of the doctors met an untimely death. One died of a heart attack shortly after he testified; another developed leukemia; the third was shot to death during a robbery.

Pretty convincing stuff. Still, I believe it would be a mis-take to conclude from such examples that *all* illnesses come from a disrespect for God's Law. While there undoubtedly *is* a relationship between the two, simple common sense tells us that this relationship does not account for *all* illness. If a person insists on venturing out into snowy weather in nothing but shorts and sandals, he's setting himself up for a bout with pneumonia. If you're sitting next to a person at the office who's suffering from a bad cold, and he or she sneezes often enough, airborne viruses will probably make their way into your respiratory system—regardless of your spiritual condition.

Thus, while I stand firm in my belief that illness often is related to the state of one's spiritual well-being, it does not logically follow that I must believe *all* illness is caused in this fashion. A careful analysis of other factors—which I'll outline throughout this book—will best determine the actual cause of an illness.

If spiritual health is tied to physical health, why are so many Christians sick? There appear to be two possible answers to this question. One explanation focuses on the specific causes of an illness. For instance, medical research has linked smoking, drinking, promiscuous sexual activity, drug use, and a host of other activities to various physical illnesses. Christians, in obedience to Scripture's general teaching on these disease-producing practices, avoid them. How, then, can a Christian still get sick? He or she already is avoiding the very things that are most likely to result in some illnesses.

The problem is, while most Christians studiously avoid cigarettes, vodka, and single's bars, many don't pay the slightest bit of attention to *attitudes* that can produce illness. In the next several chapters, we'll examine how attitudes such as hatred, guilt, fear, and discontent can wreak havoc on a person's body. All such emotions are, at their source, un-Christlike, and are all reliably documented sources of illness.

What does this finding imply? Well, if a Christian is avoiding the types of food, drink, or sexual activity that can lead to physical illness, that individual still needs to examine his or her *heart*. Is some unconfessed emotional problem or harmful attitude gnawing away at you? That could well be the source of your illness. Believe me, this problem afflicts even the most sincere Christians.

S.I. McMillen tells the story of a missionary to India who was concerned about the immoral conditions in that nation. She prayed constantly about them, but remained angry at public officials who allowed such practices as child prostitution to go unpunished.

Let us assume this missionary was perfectly justified in resenting these unconcerned officials. Still, her resentment was starting to take a physical toll on her. Her anger tightened up the muscular ring at the outlet of her stomach and increased the acid output; she developed an ulcer. As her feelings of resentment continued unabated, the ulcer started bleeding. Here was a fine Christian woman who loved the Lord, had sacrificed material possessions to come to India, and who was in full-time service for Christ. Yet her feelings of resentment had produced an ulcer that on one occasion bled for six straight days, almost causing her to bleed to death—a horrible fate known as exsanguination.

By altering a few details, this same story could be told of many other Christians. They may not have bleeding ulcers, but cancer, arthritis, and a slew of other diseases have been tied to emotional turmoil. Professions of faith made in church services are not sufficient. A daily crucifixion of self and obedience to God's commands are the ingredients needed for true health.

A second possible explanation for why righteous people suffer is a bit more complicated. In fact, in considering this explanation, we are compelled to move beyond the realm of what we can know and see in our own wisdom; we must venture out onto the plane of faith.

The problem of why bad things happen to good people is a quandary that theologians and philosophers have wrestled with for centuries. And after all these years of debate, man is no closer to a definitive and agreed-upon answer than when he first began.

I am sure we've all known Christians who are vibrant in their faith, who set an example of what it means to know the indwelling Christ. And yet, without warning, these same believers become paralytics, or the victims of heart attacks or Addisons' disease.

Oh, there *are* explanations for why these things happen. God does use such circumstances for His glory. In the final analysis, though, we must commit this problem to faith. This solution is not a cop-out, nor is it an abdication of responsibility. It is simply a frank admission that there are issues in life which our finite minds cannot grasp or capture. An infinite God has promised that *all* things will work together for good for those who love Him (Rom. 8:28). That promise is not a hypothesis. It is not a theory. It is a fact, and we must treat it as such. God has entrusted us with the problem of pain. We must live with our lack of knowledge concerning it until that day when all mysteries are explained.

What conclusions can we make about the health of non-Christians? If spiritual health relates directly to one's physical well-being, what can we say about the health of persons who do not have a relationship with Jesus Christ? Is it safe to conclude that they will not enjoy a level of health comparable to that of Christians'?

This obviously is a sticky subject, one that is not easily nailed down. Examples abound of robust and hardy nonbelievers. That prominent atheist philosopher and author, Bertrand Russell, lived to be ninety-eight. George Bernard Shaw, a playwright who was not known for his love of Christianity, lived to be ninety-four. If God punishes the wicked for their spiritual disobedience, how can men like these live to a ripe old age? Perhaps David was commenting on this incongruous state of affairs when he noted that the wicked seem to "prosper at all times" (Ps. 10:5, NASB).

Actually, to answer this question it is necessary to document *general trends* rather than deviations from them. For example, most health professionals counsel their patients to avoid smoking and drinking. Yet every now and then, we hear reports of some grizzled old gent who, on turning 100, attributes his longevity to his drinking a shot of bourbon every night before bed. He also notes that he still enjoys a good cigar after dinner. Does this report mean that doctors have been universally mistaken in prescribing abstinence from such things? Should we all run out and start downing glasses of Wild Turkey and puffing on Dutch Masters to live longer? Of course not! The fact is, this one elderly gentleman's longevity is an exception to the rule about practices that affect one's life span. But it in no way invalidates the general truth of that rule. Exceptions *do* occur.

To return to my original point, then, I believe it is possible to conclude that persons who are spiritually disobedient *can* live long, healthy lives. But as a rule, I'm willing to argue that their physical health probably will not be as good as a Christian's.

How can I make such a rash statement? Consider one basic truth. The person who does not have a personal relationship with Christ can jog, swim, or skate his way to physical fitness. He can pump iron to his heart's content. He can adopt any program he wants to repair his body. Still, one stark fact remains: These efforts to improve the body do nothing to repair the soul. Men cannot reconcile themselves to God by decreasing their blood pressure or increasing their circulation. Only a recognition and appropriation of Christ's sacrificial death can bring men to God.

What's my point? Physical exercise is fine; but true physical wholeness also is dependent on the state of one's spiritual life (1 Tim. 4:7-8). I've seen this phenomenon too many times to doubt its truth.

In 1980, I spent several weeks working in a hospital in the Central African Republic. While I was there, many of the women told me they worried about their ability to bear children—and with good reason. Some research turned up the fact that a shockingly high infertility rate existed among the women of the Zande tribe.

One reason for this statistic was related to their lifestyle. In order to prove themselves desirable as potential wives, Zande women try to develop as many sexual partners as possible. Yet as a result of their promiscuity, many of them contract pelvic inflammatory disease—an infection which leads to infertility. Such infections scar the delicate tissue of the fallopian tubes, rendering conception nearly impossible.

God's warning in Deuteronomy 25:15-18 had been visited on these women. Because of their wayward living, they were suffering from the curse of the barren womb. This may seem a rather harsh conclusion to reach. Then again, sin always has harsh results. These women had heard the message of salvation, but were determined to stick to their own way of living.

A similar choice is ours: We can follow God and life, or we can opt for sin and death. God's prescription for health is waiting for all who choose to take it. It is, indeed, the breath of life.

A Word about Physical Exercise

In the opening paragraphs of this chapter, I made a few comments about the value of physical exercise. Before we get too far into the topic of spiritual health, perhaps I should make one or two clarifying remarks about my feelings concerning bodily exercise.

First, I'm not saying that we never should exercise. I'm not advocating that we allow our bodies to deteriorate. Far from it. In fact, the *Journal of the American Medical Association* has concluded that being physically fit helps protect against hypertension and heart attack. So please don't misunderstand me. You don't have to burn your sweat suit or toss out your running shoes.

Second, the guidelines many fitness experts recommend for improving your body's health actually can have important—and unexpected—*spiritual* applications. If we could summarize the specialists' advice, we'd find that for the body to function effectively, we must practice five habits of good health.

1. *Regular exercise.* This recommendation will not surprise anyone who hasn't been living in a cave for the last twenty years. It also explains why health clubs, fitness spas, and sports centers have been springing up recently like teepees in an Indian settlement.

2. *Regular diet.* If you have never been placed on a restricted diet—the type that regulates your intake of salt, cholesterol, sugar, and similar items—you probably know someone who has. You're also probably familiar with the confused look that characterizes the person on the diet ("What type of salt, if any, can I take? How much? How often? Can I eat food with cholesterol? Does fiber prevent cancer or cause it?").

3. *Regular elimination.* This refers to the most normal of all human processes: the trip to the bathroom. Unless our systems are kept clean—either by natural or artificial means—we'll suffer the same fate as clogged sewer pipes.

4. *Regular vacations.* There seems to be a general perception in our society that one week of vacation in Florida can add a year to a person's life. While the medical verdict on that claim is still out, most physicians *do* agree that the body needs time to recuperate from the stress we place on it during the other fifty-one weeks of the year.

5. *Regular checkups.* At least once a year, to ensure that your earthly temple isn't about to fall apart, doctors recommend a checkup. This experience can consist of such procedures as having X rays, mammograms, EKGs, and some seventy-two compounds in your blood analyzed. Once you're through being poked and probed, you'll be ready for that week in Florida!

A Spiritual Prescription

Having examined these prescriptions for *physical* fitness, let's now outline their *spiritual* fitness corollaries.

1. *Spiritual exercise.* Is Scripture memorization the metaphysical equivalent of jogging? Maybe not. But there's no doubt that for our spirits to be healthy, we must subject them to the same rugged discipline swimmers, baseball players, and skiers do their bodies. Prayer, devotional reading, and regular fellowship with a body of believers all should be a part of our spiritual regimen. While it's always tempting to "take the low road" and stay in bed on Sunday morning, we need to remember that a world-class athlete never misses an opportunity to sharpen his or her skills. Neither should we.

2. *Spiritual diet.* Instead of spending every waking moment counting our carbohydrate, fat, and sugar intake, we all would do well to spend time concentrating on our spiritual diet. What's your soul been consuming lately: Hollywood's latest offerings, or the enriching nutrition of God's Word? Memorizing and incorporating the timeless principles of the Word into our lives is a key to true spiritual—and, in turn, physical—health.

3. *Confession.* Just as your digestive tract must eliminate waste materials, your soul must eliminate unconfessed sin, hatred, greed, bitterness, and pride. As we'll see in later chapters, spiritual confession is just as vital to physical health as regular elimination—if not more so.

4. *Celebration and thanksgiving.* I've seen people spend an entire year planning for a two-week vacation. While vacations *are* important, we should remember that the spiritual corollary of a regular vacation is the observance of regular times of celebration and thanksgiving to God. If we are to have healthy souls, we must devote a part of each day to seeking God in prayer, meditation, and rest. By thanking Him for His many blessings, we will see noticeable improvements in both our physical and spiritual health. Indeed, "A joyful heart is good medicine" (Prov. 17:22, NASB).

5. *Spiritual inventory.* If we can afford the time and expense of yearly medical checkups, would it not seem wise to invest some time, energy, and honesty in performing checkups of our souls? Monitor your spirit's "vital signs": Are

you getting enough spiritual exercise, or are you saddled with a flabby faith? Are you on a junk-food diet when it comes to the care and feeding of your soul?

Here's a simple chart that summarizes the correlations between physical and spiritual fitness.

PHYSICAL FITNESS		SPIRITUAL FITNESS
REGULAR EXERCISE	——	SPIRITUAL EXERCISE
REGULAR DIET	——	SPIRITUAL DIET
REGULAR ELIMINATION	——	CONFESSION
REGULAR VACATIONS	——	CELEBRATION & THANKSGIVING
REGULAR CHECK-UPS	——	SPIRITUAL INVENTORY

In looking at God's prescription for spiritual health, we should recognize at least one important fact. Basically, our society's concept of what makes for health and well-being differs from our Lord's. Maintaining an absolutely perfect diet, vacationing in the most exotic of locales, and having your body examined by the entire staff of the Mayo Clinic may do something for your health—but unless you're also actively involved in a regular program of spiritual fitness you can't realize your full potential!

The five points outlined here should only be considered *introductory* steps to spiritual fitness. They're certainly not the whole story. In later chapters, we'll develop more extensive guidelines to help you attain a better level of spiritual health. We'll also closely examine the types of spiritual attitudes that contribute to poor physical health.

Chapter Two
Beneath the Deepest Sea

I laid down an absorbable suture, left the operating room, and relaxed at the recovery-room desk to write postoperative orders. Another infected appendix—that finger-shaped appendage made of lymphoid tissue—had been removed. Another fourteen-year-old boy had a scar to show and a story to tell.

My next operation, an exploratory, was to start in thirty minutes. I had planned to use the time to talk with the boy's parents and to handle some administrative chores. But before I even had an opportunity to finish writing the orders, a nurse came up to me and delivered an urgent message.

"There's a man sitting out in the emergency room who's crying his eyes out. No one seems to know what's wrong with him, and he won't tell anyone what his trouble is. He just keeps saying it's important that he see you. Do you want to talk to him?"

I nodded my head. I knew who it was.

I walked through the double doors that led to the emergency room and saw him sitting there. I had been treating Stan as a patient in my private practice for several years.

"How are you today, Stan?" I asked, seating myself next to him, already knowing I'd posed the wrong question.

"I don't know how much longer I can go on like this."

"Are you still drinking?"

A pause, a sniffle. "Uh-huh."

Stan was a middle-aged husband, father, and alcoholic. His weakness for alcohol had, predictably, created a number of problems in his life. As a husband, his drinking had caused his wife endless worry, sorrow, and misery. As a father, his drinking had alienated him from his teenaged daughter, who desperately needed his attention. As a warehouse dispatcher, his drinking had him missing time from work and getting into scrapes with his coworkers. Stan was aware of the consequences of his drinking. He knew the fine line he was treading. Still, he continued to drink more. The obvious question was, why? If he knew what he was doing to himself and to those around him, why did he persist on this self-destructive course?

The source of Stan's problem, I believe, can be summed up in one word: guilt.

Stan essentially viewed himself as a failure. For years, he had considered himself both a poor father and husband—and he felt *guilty* about that. As a result, he sought refuge in alcohol's numbing embrace. Yet in doing so, he was simply perpetuating a vicious circle: Feeling guilty about his personal inadequacies, he would drink; then feeling guilty about his excessive drinking, he'd drink more in an effort to forget this guilt. All throughout this process, despite my pleading, he refused God's forgiveness. And, I suspect, Stan felt guilty about that too.

Guilt. It's a disease of staggering proportions, a disease whose effects I doubt few people fully understand. If you were to visit the mental institutions of our country, you'd find that guilt is the source of numerous patients' problems. Of the 385 beds in the hospital at which I work, a full 10 percent are occupied by people suffering from various forms of mental illness. And based on the stories many of these mental patients tell, one fact is clear: Many are in the hospital because of unresolved, festering guilt in their lives.

The Source of Guilt

Guilt is not a recent discovery of psychology; it's not an emotion indigenous only to twentieth-century man. I was talking with a young college student, a psychology major, about this subject the other day. His comments were revealing.

"Oh, guilt," he said. "That's a very Freudian concept. You know psychologists are just beginning to understand that guilt is the by-product of man's failure to come to grips with life in an industrialized and alienated society." Uh, right.

Actually, the roots of guilt are much clearer. This emotion is a sense of remorse produced by the knowledge that we have broken a rule or a law. Of course, many of us use the term *guilt* in a loose sort of way to describe a variety of emotions. We fail to call Mom on Mother's Day and feel "guilty" about our negligence. We speak harshly to a friend and are hounded by "guilt."

For the purposes of our study, though, we will focus on that aspect of guilt which results specifically from a conscious violation of *God's* Law. Scripture indicates that God has given His people certain laws by which to live. He also has given us a built-in ability—our conscience—to determine when we have broken one of those statutes. I know that sounds very unscientific, but the violation of God's Law—sin—is an event which occurs in a spiritual dimension, not in a laboratory.

Our ability to accurately recognize guilt is well documented in Scripture. David, for example, chronicles his reaction to the knowledge that he's broken one of God's commands:

> When I kept silent, my bones wasted away through
> my groaning all day long. For day and night Your
> hand was heavy upon me (Ps. 32:3-4).

There's no two ways about it. David had sinned, tried to cover it up, and now was feeling a sense of remorse—or guilt—about this whole affair. But was his guilt the result of a "failure to come to grips with life in an industrialized and alienated society"? Hardly.

David realized that his sin (which was due to his immoral relationship with Bathsheba) was a direct violation of God's Law concerning adultery. The Lord made David acutely aware of his transgression. As God spoke to this ex-shepherd, David's "built-in ability" to recognize a violation of the Lord's Law was activated. His conscience was sensitized. He felt guilt. And that guilt caused a number of unpleasant physical side effects in his life. Look at his words again:"My bones wasted away through my groaning. . . . Your hand was heavy on me." How would you like to have the hand of the infinite God—the God who created heaven and earth—on *you?*

In David's case, guilt occurred because he disavowed a moral standard that God had established. When men and women ignore those standards today by engaging, for instance, in premarital intercourse, guilt also can result. The essentials of holy living haven't changed over the last 3,000 years.

I recently spoke with a young woman who had been taught that sex was to occur only within the context of marriage. Yet for one evening she had ignored that rule, had a brief affair with a young man, and now was regretting it deeply. "All my life I dreamed I'd be a virgin on my wedding night," she cried. "Now that chance is gone forever. And I feel so ashamed, so guilty about it."

The fact is, God has established certain biblical standards—all of which are clearly explained in His Word—which, if broken, will convict us of our having trespassed against Him. We disobey these standards whenever we opt for the worlds' brand of happiness over God's command for us to live "in this world, but not of it." We disobey His Law when we forsake commitment and sacrifice to spiritual matters to seek material advancement. We violate His commands when we adopt the attitude that we have a certain *right* to do as we please, whenever we please.

As with David, and also with the young woman who shared her shattered dream with me, when we disobey God, His heavy hand comes to rest on us. Guilt makes it abundantly clear—if we're honest with ourselves—that we are estranged from Him.

Our Responses to Guilt

Once this feeling of remorse comes upon us, we can react in a number of ways. Obviously, God would have us respond to our guilt in a healthy and straightforward manner. This involves confessing our sin. If we admit to God that we've violated His standards, "He is faithful and just and will forgive us our sins and purify us from all unrighteousness" (1 John 1:9). We'll more fully discuss the need for confession and God's forgiving grace later in this chapter.

I postpone this discussion of forgiveness for one reason. Unfortunately, many people do *not* respond to their feelings of guilt in the way God desires. Instead, they respond in a way that widens the gulf between themselves and Him, deepens their sense of guilt, and often leads to serious physical problems. For all these reasons, it's important that we spend some time documenting the ruinous effects of guilt.

Our failure to deal with guilt in a healthy manner can assume one of four basic forms.

Rebellion. Pete's parents were Christians, and as well as they could, they tried to instill a sense of Christian values in their son's life. Yet occasionally Pete would sneak off behind his parents' backs and go out drinking with his friends. Pete realized that what he was doing contradicted a number of spiritual principles, and he'd usually regret his behavior. But soon, after more and more prodding and encouragement from his friends, Pete began to wonder why he should feel sorry about what he did. He was eighteen; he was an adult. *Forget these guilt pangs,* he decided. *I'll do whatever I want!* Before long, Pete was drinking regularly—and heavily.

In essence, Pete had responded to his guilt feelings by

rebelling against standards he intuitively knew were correct. Rather than admitting that his behavior was displeasing to God, he hardened his heart and ran headlong into a lifestyle that he thought could insulate him from his guilt.

Judgmentalism. Another way to deal with our guilt is to *deny* that we're feeling any sense of remorse. Instead, we compare our behavior to others; if we can convince ourselves that other people behave at least as poorly as we do, perhaps we won't feel so badly about our own actions. Maybe our guilt will pass.

This particular response to guilt is hardly new. In fact, Adam first tried it out in the Garden of Eden. When God confronted him with the fact that he had eaten fruit from the tree of knowledge, Adam knew the Lord had him red-handed. But how did Adam react? Shrewdly, he blamed Eve: "She gave me some fruit from the tree, and I ate it" (Gen. 3:12).

Can you believe it? Adam has just plunged all of mankind into sin, and he has the audacity to tell God, "Hey, don't be mad at *me.* Eve gave me the fruit. How was *I* supposed to know it was forbidden? I've got nothing to feel guilty about."

Unfortunately, Adam's strategy for dealing with guilt has been passed down through the generations. We've now become quite effective practitioners of it. If we neglect to attend regular worship services, we can rationalize our guilt away by saying, "Yeah, I haven't been to church in two months, but the Johnsons haven't gone in *three!*"

Lowered self-esteem. Do the words, "I've sinned, I feel like a worm," ring a bell? Perhaps the most widely practiced response to sin-inspired guilt is to feel utterly worthless. This particular response reflects the flip side of the "rebellion" response. Rather than thumbing our noses at God and our guilt, we cave in under the weight of His "heavy hand."

In his first epistle, John says he is writing his letter "so that you will not sin" (1 John 2:1). By logical extension, it's also clear John is writing this epistle so that his readers will not experience the guilt which sin produces. John obviously was aware that many believers experience severe guilt when they sin. So he quickly adds, "But if anybody does sin we have One who speaks to the Father in our defense" (v. 2). Regrettably, many people never get past John's injunction in 2:1. All they see is the admonition not to sin. Then, when they do violate a biblical standard—and feel guilty over doing so—they conclude, "I've fallen again. God can't possibly love me. I'm a spiritual washout."

Isolation. The fourth general reaction to guilt usually is an outgrowth of lowered self-esteem. Basically, an individual, feeling guilty for having trespassed against God, withdraws into his or her self. This was Stan's problem. While his reaction to guilt contained elements of rebellion (he continued drinking and refused God's forgiveness), his primary problem was that he withdrew from his contacts with God, his family, and his coworkers in order to wrestle with his personal demons. The results of this type of self-imposed isolation can be devastating.

The Physical Consequences of Guilt

To this point, we've seen how the presence of guilt in our lives can produce a number of attitudinal responses. These various attitudes, however, do not exist in a vacuum; they cannot occur without affecting other aspects of our personhood. It should come as no surprise, then, that guilt can have demonstrable effects on our physical health.

Let's examine a few of these bodily responses to guilt.

The consequences of rebellion. When Pete decided to turn his back on God, deny the presence of guilt in his life, and embark on a life of dissipation, he thought he was teaching God a lesson. He'd show the Lord of the universe that he could run from Him and have a great time to boot.

Pete was only fooling himself. By increasing his intake of alcohol—and later, drugs—he was entering his body in a demolition derby. This is a common response to guilt: to adopt an extremely reckless lifestyle. But what are some of the consequences of this choice?

In Shakespeare's classic play *Othello,* one character exclaims: "O God! That men should put an enemy in their mouths to steal away their brains." In this instance, in addition to his vast literary talents, the bard also displayed a fairly good understanding of the biological effects of alcohol on the human brain. Because liquor produces areas of atrophy in the brain, a number of chronic alcoholics *do* develop insanity in some form. Their brains *are,* figuratively, stolen away.

I'm sorry to report, however, that the effects of alcohol aren't limited solely to our gray matter. One out of five alcoholics also develops partial muscular paralysis and many others complain of painful neuritis.

Drinking also leads to hardening of the liver—and when blood from the gastrointestinal tract is prevented from flowing freely through a hardened liver, built up pressure in the veins may cause the abdominal cavity to distend with fluid. In many cases, the obstructed liver also can cause back pressure and ballooning of the veins of the esophagus. These thinned-out veins can rupture and may result in serious or fatal hemorrhaging.

As for drug use, almost all nonmedicinal drugs or narcotics are harmful to the body in one way or another. Cocaine use, for example, can lead to manifest personality disorders, high blood pressure, and the total destruction of the lining of the nasal passage. Even marijuana, which is considered the least harmful illegal drug, can produce subtle personality changes after prolonged use. Recent studies have shown too that the use of marijuana can, if used often enough, lead to possible gene damage and hormonal imbalance in one's own body or in an offspring.

By now, the relationship between cigarette smoking and cancer is well established. But many people don't realize that chronic lung disease—which also can be caused by smoking—results in lower oxygen levels in the blood and predisposes a person to heart attack.

Smoking and overeating also can contribute to a devastat-

ing condition knows as atherosclerosis. This condition occurs when cholesterol, a yellowish waxy substance, is depos-
ited on the inside surface of the arteries, including the
arteries of the neck leading to the brain, as well as those
which supply blood to the heart muscle. Sometimes cholesterol narrows the major artery which carries oxygenated
blood from the heart to other parts of the body diminishing
blood supply to the chest, abdomen, arms, and legs.

Eventually, affected arteries become scarred and inlaid
with deposits of fibrous-like materials and calcium. Hemor-
rhages may occur just beneath the inside surface of the
arteries, or clots may form in the remaining narrow open-
ings. Pathologists who performed autopsies on American
soldiers killed during the Korean War found that many of
these young men had arteries so completely clogged with
cholesterol that only a small opening remained through
which blood could pass. If they hadn't died in combat,
atherosclerosis surely would have killed them.

Obviously, all of these diseases are not necessarily the
result of guilt. Atherosclerosis can occur in the arteries of the
most guilt-free saint. Still, it seems clear that when a person
responds to guilt by adopting an intemperate, and or rebel-
lious lifestyle, such behavior dramatically increases his
chances for developing one or more of these conditions.

The consequences of judgmentalism. Our propensity to
deflect our feelings of guilt by judging others' behavior
simply dulls our moral perceptions of what's right and what's
wrong. Instead of working to resolve our problems, we
burrow deeper into a rut of self-deception. And while we
may be able to fool our minds for a few weeks or months, we
can't fool our bodies indefinitely. Sooner or later, our bodies
will react to all of the suppressed emotional turmoil we've
allowed to build up inside.

Frank had been feeling guilty over his decision to pursue a
lucrative career as a chemical engineer. What was there to
feel guilty about? Well, he had promised God early in his
college career that he'd use his training to secure work in a

Muslim nation. Since Christian missionaries aren't allowed in most Islamic countries, but engineers are, Frank hoped to use his education as a means to gain entry into one of these nations. Once there, he could discreetly witness to his Muslim coworkers. But when a major chemical firm offered Frank a job in the States shortly after graduation, he experienced a change of heart.

"It just seemed too good an offer to turn down," he later told me. "Besides, a lot of my other friends had noble ideals that they deserted for good paying jobs. What was I supposed to do? Miss out on all the action when none of my friends were?"

Ah, that was the rub. Frank was feeling guilty about his decision; but he was weighing his actions against those of his friends in order to rationalize his guilt. Now he was sitting in my office, suffering from the first symptoms of toxic goiter. His repressed feelings had caused an excess of thyroxin to pour into his blood over the last several months. This resulted in his developing extreme nervousness, bulging eyes, and a rapid pulse. If he continues to harbor his guilt, he eventually could develop fatal heart disease.

The consequences of lowered self-esteem. The most obvious physical consequence of a poor self-image is depression. That's right: depression is a physical condition, as well as an emotional one. In fact, there are so many physical implications to depression, a later chapter will deal with this problem more completely.

Depression, if taken to its most tragic extreme, can lead to suicide. And suicide, to put it bluntly, is the ultimate physical response to a spiritually based problem.

The consequences of isolation. When people respond to guilt by withdrawing into themselves, by curling into a life of loneliness, strange things happen to their bodies. In *The Broken Heart,* Dr. James Lynch, a medical researcher at Johns Hopkins, sets forth a remarkable theory. Dr. Lynch strongly believes that loneliness is the number one physical killer in America today. A decade of research has shown, he says, that those who withdraw from other people have premature death rates from two to ten times higher than sociable individuals. Dr. Lynch's studies show that twice as many white males under age seventy who live a solitary lifestyle die from heart disease, lung cancer, and stomach cancer. Three times as many men in this category die of hypertension and seven times as many from cirrhosis of the liver.

While these figures were based primarily on research documenting the physiological responses of single, divorced, and widowed persons, one fact does shine through: prolonged isolation is not healthy. And if guilt causes us to withdraw from others, these same physical problems could very well come to plague us.

God's Prescription for Guilt

The various diseases we've examined in this chapter are not always caused by guilt. Other factors do produce them. However, for each of the four categories of guilt-related illnesses we've discussed, the specific illnesses cited were but a small percentage of *possible* guilt-induced diseases.

As a doctor, I can treat these diseases. I can operate on you to repair an ulcer or prescribe a medication to reduce the level of thyroxin in your blood. Still, wouldn't it be simpler, more effective, and less costly to allow God to cure your guilt before I have to start working on you?

So what *is* God's prescription for guilt? We simply need to confess the sin that is causing our guilt, repent of it, and accept His forgiveness.

Some folks labor under the misguided opinion that a little guilt now and then never hurt anyone. In light of the medical data presented in this chapter, we know such a claim is false. Not once does the Bible encourage Christians to wallow in their guilt. Not once are Christians commanded to rebel against guilt or to suffer from a sense of worthlessness because of it.

God offers His prescription for the dilemma of human guilt

through the sacrificial death of His Son. By appropriating the benefits of Christ's death on our behalf, we can have a spiritually and physically healthy alternative to guilt: forgiveness. The sin which has led to our guilt can be washed away.

Our Lord's forgiving nature and His willingness to forgive are well documented in Scripture. In the Book of Acts alone we read:

> All the prophets testify about Him that everyone who believes in Him receives forgiveness of sins (Acts 10:43).

> Therefore, my brothers, I want you to know that through Jesus the forgiveness of sins is proclaimed to you (13:38).

> They may receive forgiveness of sins and a place among those who are sanctified by faith in Me (26:18).

These verses can become real only after we have experienced them. Whenever we ask God, through Christ, for forgiveness of sin, we *can* be released from the weight of guilt and its physically debilitating side effects. After a few moments of honest prayer and confession, a divine fitness can fill your mind and body. Why would anyone want to suffer from guilt when forgiveness is but a prayer away?

Between 1958 and 1962, I completed my internship and surgical residency at Gorgas Hospital in the Panama Canal Zone. While there, I visited a prison that had been built by conquering Spaniards several centuries earlier. This prison was unique for a number of reasons. First, it was built directly on the shoreline of the Pacific Ocean; second, its cells all faced toward the water. There was a particular reason for this interesting construction.

You see, in Panama, tides can reach a height of thirteen feet. They completely cover the shore and don't go out for hours. The Spaniards placed their prisoners in the jail's cells when the tide was out. Then, as the tide came in, the entire cell—with the prisoner locked inside—was flooded with water. Guards emptied the cells of lifeless bodies after the tide had gone out again.

Can you imagine the unspeakable terror those prisoners felt as the tide came in, as the water rose higher and higher and they knew they had no way to escape?

A person experiencing guilt may feel much like the prisoner in that cell. Guilt may be rising around him and he feels as though there's no way out. But thanks to God, He has provided us with the forgiveness necessary to eradicate the sin which produces our guilt. We can burst free from our prison cells!

If we take this prescription today, and renew our spiritual health, God will remove our guilt "as far as the east is from the west" (Ps. 103:12). He will bury our sins beneath the deepest sea (Micah 7:19). We can be assured that guilt will never be a source of physical illness in our lives.

Chapter Three
Lost Rights

John Hunter should have known better. As one of the eighteenth century's leading anatomists and surgeons, Hunter knew he suffered from a congenitally weak heart. He also knew that whenever he became angry, he was placing a tremendous strain on this vital organ. On one occasion, in fact, he even remarked, "The first scoundrel that gets me angry will kill me."

Despite his knowledge of how anger could affect his body, Hunter apparently chose to ignore that fact. He went right on being angry whenever he felt the situation warranted it. One day, however, while verbally attacking an opponent at a medical conference, Hunter suddenly gripped his chest and crumpled to the floor. His angry outburst had caused such a contraction of the blood vessels in his heart that the muscle simply stopped pumping. John Hunter was dead, killed by his own anger.

As this example demonstrates, anger is an emotion with clear physical ramifications. James apparently appreciated this connection, for in his epistle he advises believers to avoid anger:

> Everyone should be quick to listen, slow to speak
> and slow to become angry (James 1:19).

The Apostle Paul repeatedly includes anger and hatred among the types of behavior Christians should renounce:

> We lived in malice and envy, being hated and hating one another (Titus 3:3).

> The acts of the sinful nature are . . . hatred . . . fits of rage (Gal. 5:19-20).

> Get rid of all bitterness, rage and anger (Eph. 4:31).

And Job sums up exactly why anger is such a deadly emotion: "Resentment kills a fool" (Job 5:2).

So what *is* anger? Like many other emotions, we use this one word to describe a variety of moods. We may say we feel "angry" over the situation in the Middle East. Or, as in Hunter's case, we're "angry" because someone disagrees with us.

Webster defines anger as "a strong feeling of displeasure." Yet for the housewife who's just discovered the kids have tracked mud all over her freshly polished kitchen floor, a sanitized dictionary definition just can't capture the width and depth of this emotion. Perhaps, then, because anger is such a many-splendored thing, *Roget's Thesaurus* lists at least fourteen different synonyms for anger—from the comparatively mild *resentment* to the more demonstrative *fury*.

Given this wealth of definitions and sources of anger, we'd do well to focus on some specific aspects of anger, including the *spiritual* dimensions of anger. What is it about man's spiritual condition that makes anger, resentment, and hatred such common emotions?

What Causes Anger?

An often-ignored cause of anger can be summed up in two words: lost rights.

As a result of the Fall, all men "have sinned, and come

short of the glory of God" (Rom. 3:23, KJV). As a consequence of Adam's sin, you and I have inherited his sinful disposition, are estranged from God, and can be reunited with Him only through a personal relationship with Jesus Christ. This theological truth tells us a great deal about why people get angry. As sinners, we're basically intent on pursuing our own interests over and above anything and everything else. As Isaiah put it, "Each of us has turned to his own way" (Isa. 53:6). Most of us feel we have an absolute, albeit intangible, *right* to do or possess certain things.

When we feel as though someone or something has kept us from exercising our inalienable rights, we respond by lashing out at them. If someone pricks the bubble in which our self-centered world has been floating, we feel as if our rights have been violated. We respond with anger.

This may seem a rather odd way to analyze anger. But if we break this emotion down into a few easy-to-examine components, we'll see that the notion of "lost rights" actually explains a fair amount of our angry behavior. I believe this concept also will show us how anger can have deleterious effects on our earthly temples.

The Right to Do Things "My Way"

A pastor once told me that whenever he heard the old Frank Sinatra song, "My Way," he cringed. It's not that he had anything personal against Mr. Sinatra. It's just that the basic message of this song—"Through it all, I did it *my way*"—captures the very attitude that places so many patients in my office.

You see, one of the "rights" most individuals feel they possess is the right to live in whatever manner they please. This right can be manifested in any number of ways. Some folks want to live life in the fast lane, with no mention of God or sin. Others may think they're entitled to manipulate the lives of family members or coworkers. At the base of such attitudes, though, is the selfish sin nature.

But in a world where "no man is an island," there inevitably comes a time when the pursuit of "my way" runs smack into someone or something that says, "No. You can't have it." When that happens, watch out! Someone's "rights" have been violated and the world is going to know about it. Unfortunately, this person's angry response probably will reach his own digestive tract before it gets to anyone else's ears.

Del was in my office several years ago. If ever there was an individual who liked to see things done his way, it was Del. On this particular occasion, he was seeing me because he was suffering from diarrhea mixed with blood and mucous, which usually is a symptom of colitis.

"When did you start experiencing discomfort?" I asked.

I could see Del starting to do a slow boil. "That wife of mine," he sputtered. "All I wanted to do was plant a little vegetable garden in our yard and she wouldn't let me. She said it would decrease our property value and make our house look tacky."

"But Del, you've got a very small backyard as it is. Where were you planning to start this garden?"

"Oh, I thought I'd put it out in *front* of the house. But no! She wouldn't let me!"

Obviously, to Del, the irrationality of his wanting to grow tomatoes and corn in his front yard was not the problem. For him, the fact that he wanted to do something *his way,* and his wife was violating that right, was making him furious.

Flare-ups of ulcerative colitis often are caused and perpetuated by the very type of anger Del was experiencing. Ulcers are an even more common by-product of anger. When the body is subjected to an agitated state for an extended period of time, excess acid pours into the stomach, and digestion of live tissue results. That old expression, "He's eating himself up inside," is more accurate than most people realize.

The Right to Possessions
Some people have turned their possessions into gods. They

worship their homes, their cars, their stereo systems. Woe to anyone who tries to come between such an individual and his prized possession.

In the parable of the unmerciful servant, we read of a man who was so attached to his money that he had a fellow servant thrown into prison because of a bad debt (Matt. 18:21-35). Obviously, the unmerciful servant figured he had a right to his possessions, and no deadbeat was going to violate that right. His attitude reflected a sinful selfishness.

In the United States, our belief in our right to possessions becomes particularly evident around April 15. At that time, we practice the solemn custom of bundling up a good portion of our yearly income and sending it off to live with its rich uncle in Washington. It also is no coincidence that around this time of year, family practioners see quite a few high blood pressure cases. The sad truth is, some people just get so attached to their earthly possessions—those things which moths and rust destroy (Matt. 6:19)—that they get downright angry when they're forced to part with them.

If these people knew what their high blood pressure was doing to them, they might think twice before flying off the handle. High blood pressure causes the muscular "coats" around the arteries to flex into a continual state of excessive tension. As a result, the arteries narrow and the blood flow is restricted. Eventually, the arterial walls become permanently thickened, or "hypertrophied," making the narrowed passageways a permanent feature of the circulatory system.

Long-term high blood pressure also results in heart damage (as the heart pumps at a too-high pressure, the walls of the heart tend to thicken and enlarge) and kidney failure (high blood pressure reduces the blood flow in the kidneys, leading to progressive damage and a decreased ability to rid the bloodstream of waste products).

The Right to Health

Many people feel they have a right to health, a right that even takes precedence over their obedience to God. Perhaps the experience of a young Christian woman I was told about will help bring this concept into focus.

Denise is an office manager with an American relief agency that supplies food, medicine, and other needed supplies to Third World nations. She also is a devoted physical fitness buff. She exercises during her lunch hour, takes the daily recommended dosage of a score of vitamins, and runs five miles every day after work.

Despite her real concern for the needy in underdeveloped countries, Denise's particular responsibilities in the office had kept her from actually visiting any of the places to which her agency supplied material. And in a way, that was fine with her. You see, Denise believed she enjoyed an inalienable right to stay healthy. To her a healthy body was one of the most important things a person could possess; after all, it was the temple of God's Spirit. So by staying out of unsanitary African and Asian villages, Denise could have the best of both worlds: She could serve God—and still stay healthy.

But then one day, the unexpected happened.

Ted worked for the same relief agency as Denise, and he was the person who usually handled the agency's overseas travel assignments. But when he came down with the flu shortly before an important trip to the Dominican Republic, Denise's superior asked her to go.

"It'll be good experience for you," he told her.

Good experience? she cried to herself. *At what? Catching malaria? I don't want to sacrifice my right to stay healthy just for the sake of "experience." Let someone else go!*

Frantically, Denise came up with a thousand reasons why she couldn't go: Monthly reports needed to be finalized, she hated flying, a new vending machine was being brought in next week; as office manager, she really ought to be around to supervise its installation.

But her superior was firm in his insistence, and assured her that he would personally take charge of the new Coke machine's arrival. Now Denise was really mad. Why? Because she was convinced she possessed a right to stay healthy in the United States—where germs, snakes, and other vermin weren't nearly as plentiful.

"God," she fumed, "what's going on here? I have a *right* to stay healthy. And going to the Dominican Republic certainly is going to violate that right. Why don't You revoke my visa and we'll just forget about the whole thing?"

Several days later, despite her persuasive protests, Denise found herself overseeing the construction of temporary housing for hurricane victims in a crowded, muddy barrio.

What impact did Denise's anger have on her body? Well, during times of emotional stress—such as occur during anger—the secretion of the ovaries is affected in a variety of ways. In Denise's case, she had been so upset that her menses was over three weeks late, and she had a particularly painful period when it did arrive.

When she finally returned to the States, Denise began to realize that a splendid irony had been at work in her life. Her ill-conceived belief that she had a right to health produced the anger which actually *reduced* her health. When she finally acknowledged the sin-centered source of her anger and surrendered her supposed "right" to health, she experienced a refreshing sense of liberation and excitement. She's already bugging her superior to send her on another trip.

God's Prescription for Anger

During Denise's illness, she learned a valuable lesson in how to overcome anger. She surrendered her rights. She let God work His will in her life. You see, if our "rights" are a primary cause of anger, then acknowledging that they are centered in our own selfishness is a major step toward triumphing over this emotion. But how can we go about relinquishing our rights? How can we appropriate God's prescription for anger?

If we are willing to view anger as a spiritually based problem, a crucial first step is to take Christ's yoke upon us

(Matt. 11:30). What does this entail? Basically, it requires us to voluntarily place ourselves under God's care and control. As an ox is yoked to steer it more effectively through its work, accepting God's yoke keeps us from allowing anger to divert our energies in harmful ways. Jesus assures us that wearing His yoke—as opposed to the yoke of anger—is infinitely less burdensome (Matt. 11:29). He also promises a full and abundant life to all who follow this prescription (John 10:10). That's a promise we ought to claim, for maintaining and protecting our imagined "rights" is a terribly costly endeavor; we pay the price for our self-centeredness in a currency comprised of ulcers, colitis, and high blood pressure.

Surrendering our rights is a key to accepting God's prescription for anger. But it's not the only aspect of His prescription. When people think of a prescription, they envision a pill they can pop once for instant relief. Yet a prescription also may require a patient to undergo various types of therapy. So it is with God's prescription for anger. He has several therapeutic exercises we must go through.

Showing Forgiveness

Jennifer hadn't been able to keep any food down for several days. Every time she ate something, she vomited it up shortly thereafter. I asked her a few brief questions, and found that she was enraged at her sister. Both did professional sewing work at home, and Jennifer had recently discovered her sister was spreading false rumors about the quality of her work.

At first, you might think Jennifer had a perfect right to be angry at her sister; after all, her sibling was lying about her. But to my surprise, Jennifer told me she actually was more upset over the fact that this falsehood had disrupted her *income*. Suspecting Jennifer's products were of an inferior quality, customers weren't sending her any more work orders.

Now the physical manifestations of Jennifer's anger had become evident. This emotional upheaval had sent nerve impulses to tighten the muscular outlet of her stomach. As a result, the food she ate could not pass into her intestines and was being regurgitated.

To appropriate God's prescription for health, Jennifer must first surrender her rights to an uninterrupted income. She must realize that setting things right with her sister takes precedence over money. If she refuses to do this, her digestive problems will only be exacerbated.

The next step in Jennifer's healing process will involve her willingness to *forgive* her sister. Paul identifies forgiveness as a hallmark of genuine love:

> Be kind and compassionate to one another, forgiving each other, just as in Christ God forgave you (Eph. 4:32).

"But," you may be saying, "that doesn't apply to a situation where another person has wronged *me.*" I'm afraid it does:

> Bear with each other and forgive whatever grievances you may have against one another. Forgive as the Lord forgave you (Col. 3:13).

In these two verses, Paul draws an interesting comparison. He states that we should forgive one another because Christ first forgave *us.* And how are we to forgive? With Christ as our model, we are to forgive *totally.* This means that we don't have to rely on our own compassion or generosity to forgive others. Rather, we rely on God's limitless supply of grace. To take this divine prescription, we need only to go to God and ask Him to fill our order. And don't worry about how you'll pay for this prescription. It's free; all we have to do is take it.

I fully realize that forgiveness is not the easiest of traits to exercise. I've seen man's lack of forgiveness taken to drastic extremes. During the eight years I worked at the mission hospital at Soddo, Ethiopia, I discovered that not every thatched hut I ran across was occupied by a family. Rather, many are left vacant; at night villagers take turns watching for thieves through the huts' barely noticeable peepholes. If a thief is caught, the villagers break the culprit's upper and lower arms, as well as his upper and lower legs. In one week, I treated thirty-eight thieves who had been the recipients of this unforgiving brand of justice.

Jesus told us, "Love your enemies and pray for those who persecute you" (Matt. 5:44). In saying those words, our Saviour was outlining the basis of forgiveness. And He was not merely suggesting we try forgiveness if we *feel* like it. He was *commanding* us to be forgiving, even when it's difficult to do so.

Paul adds one last provision to this prescription. We're to forgive one another *quickly.* "Do not let the sun go down while you are still angry" (Eph. 4:26), he writes—and with good reason. As our bodies remain in an agitated state, we increase the levels of hormones flowing from our pituitary, adrenal, thyroid, and other glands—an excess of which can cause disease in any part of the body. Therefore, it's in our body's best interest to resolve our anger as soon as we can.

Taking Wrong

Right now, I can envision many of you shaking your heads, saying, "What do you mean? If someone treats me badly, or lies about me, or cheats me, I'm not supposed to get angry?" Well, yes and no.

Naturally, our first reaction to the violation of our rights *is* anger—but Scripture points out that it's how we *deal* with this feeling that determines whether we're headed for trouble. "In your anger," the psalmist tells us, "do not sin" (Ps. 4:4). In other words, God doesn't expect us to be feelingless automatons; He knows that as living, breathing, sinning beings, anger is a part of our emotional makeup. Still, He is telling us not to let this anger spin out of control and infest other areas of our behavior.

So what are we to do?

As we've already seen, a willingness to relinquish our rights and forgive others will certainly help us keep our anger from leading to physical illness. But we also should recognize the value of one other prescription for anger: being able to take the wrong done to us, rather than seeking revenge. Paul outlines this principle in 1 Corinthians. When you feel that your rights have been violated, he writes, "Why not rather be wronged? Why not rather be cheated?" (1 Cor. 6:7). In his first epistle, Peter makes the same point: "For it is commendable if a man bears up under the pain of unjust suffering" (1 Peter 2:19).

This prescription is particularly relevant in cases where we feel that our right to possessions has been violated. As the son of medical missionaries, I spent nine of my growing-up years in the Orient. One summer, our family enjoyed a vacation at a beach resort on the northern coast of China. The bungalow we rented wasn't far from the beach and we had access to a beautiful, shallow bay. While there, my father purchased a six-foot long paddleboat for our use. At the time he bought it, it looked perfect; not a flaw could be seen.

As soon as we got the boat back to the bungalow, my brother and I raced down to the bay and prepared to paddle away. I remember thinking that the boat looked as beautiful as the Titanic on the day it was christened. That comparison proved to be quite apt, for after ten minutes of use, seventeen knotholes appeared in the bottom of the boat. In short order, my brother, myself, and our new paddleboat slowly began sinking into the blue Pacific.

As my father observed this minor disaster from the shore, he naturally felt angry at the merchant who had sold him this inferior product. He also had several decisions to make, foremost of which was whether he was going to haul the merchant into court and get even with him. Personally, as I looked at my paddleboat lying half-submerged in the Chinese bay, I was all in favor of seeking some sort of revenge.

But my father did an interesting thing. He retrieved the leaky paddleboat and traded it in for another—without a single harsh word to the merchant. Though he had every right to be mad about the situation, my father didn't allow his anger to lead him into sin. Rather, he took the wrong, accepted the loss, and looked for an acceptable alternative to it. The discerning reader will understand why my father never suffered an ulcer.

Sixteen years later, I had an opportunity to test my own attitude toward being cheated. During the summer, I worked ten to twelve hours a day, six days a week, for six weeks doing house construction. I had hoped to earn enough money to pay for my sophomore tuition in medical school and to save up to marry my college sweetheart. The contractor had promised his workers that we'd all receive our pay in one lump sum at the end of the summer. That payment, however, never came; in mid-August, the builder declared bankruptcy. I found I had worked those six weeks for little more than the privilege of building experience and character. Granted, those are great traits to acquire but, at the time, my employer's dishonesty left me in a state of dismay.

A number of my coworkers decided to band together and take as much of the contractor's personal property and equipment as possible to compensate for their lost wages. They asked me if I wanted to join them. For a moment, I considered it. I was angry—*very* angry— and my rights had been violated. But then, an image of a leaky paddleboat flashed in my mind. In that instant, I knew what I had to do. I thanked my friends for their concern. As for me, I was going to take the wrong.

It wasn't naiveté that made me abandon my chance to seek legal recourse. The point is, I knew that if I got involved in a lawsuit, the anger I initially had felt over this situation would simply feed on itself. If I got involved in a lawsuit, I knew I'd mull over how unfairly I'd been treated, and my rage would increase. So I relinquished my right to what I was owed, forgave the contractor, and took the wrong. I left the matter with God and never required any medication for my anger. I only needed to take God's prescription for it. When I returned to medical school, through the Lord's provision, the money I needed eventually became available.

A Better Way

I realize there's a great deal that could be written about anger. I also realize that a number of things probably have been left unstated in this one short chapter. The subject of "righteous anger," for example, is one that fascinates me. Many people remember Jesus' scourging of the temple and conclude, "Well, if Jesus could get angry, why can't I? Doesn't that prove anger is an acceptable emotion?"

Of course, there's a tremendous difference between what motivated the Son of God's anger and what motivates man's. Basically, I think James managed to answer the question of whether there's ever a good excuse for our being angry— even in cases where we think our indignation is justified: "Man's anger does not bring about the righteous life that God desires" (James 1:20).

No, anger doesn't bring about a righteous life. It only generates more anger. And, as we've seen, it also can be a significant cause of a number of physical ailments.

Booker T. Washington, the great educator, suffered from racial discrimination throughout his life. If anyone ever had a "right" to be angry at people or circumstances, he'd certainly seem to qualify. And yet Washington said:

> I will not let any man reduce my soul to the level
> of hatred.

Shouldn't we possess that same attitude? Shouldn't we be willing to take God's prescription for anger?

Chapter Four
Worry, Worry, Worry

Everybody worries about something. How about you? Are you worried about your financial resources, anxious that you won't be able to make this month's payment on that new car? Or do you fear that you lack those abilities necessary to make you a better husband, mother, student, or pastor? Perhaps you fear the unknown. I know I often do.

When God called me as a teenager to devote my life to missionary medicine, I was fearful of where He ultimately would send me. I was afraid I'd wind up in some horrible habitat where I'd contract leprosy, tuberculosis, typhus, or typhoid. I feared I'd never find a wife who'd consent to a life of hardship overseas. All these fears were genuine, and all were fears of the unknown.

These types of fears—and many more—are common to most people. We might even consider them "normal." But there's also a class of anxieties that are a bit more offbeat; they're so unusual, in fact, that psychologists have come up with some equally unusual names for them. Here's a sampling of several of the more bizarre fears that dwell in the human heart:

- Baccillophobia—fear of bacteria
- Ballistophobia—fear of bullets

- Belonephobia—fear of needles and sharp, pointed objects
- Gephyrophobia—fear of crossing bridges
- Taphephobia—fear of being buried alive
- Trichophobia—fear of hair

Of course, fears aren't *always* a bad thing to have. Most of us suffer, for example, from a mild case of apiphobia—the fear of bees. I mean, how many of us actually run after bees, trying to provoke them into stinging us? On the whole, our fear of bees is a rather healthy trait to possess. Along these same lines, author C. Neil Strait has observed:

> Not all fears are bad. Many of them are wholesome, indeed, very necessary for life. The fear of God, the fear of fire, the fear of electricity, are life-saving fears that, if heeded, bring a new knowledge to life.

Likewise, Scripture tells us:

> The fear of the Lord is the beginning of wisdom (Prov. 9:10).

> The fear of the Lord leads to life (Prov. 19:23).

It would be nice if our fears played only those roles ascribed to them by Mr. Strait and the writer of Proverbs. We'd all probably be healthier, wealthier, and wiser in the long run. Unfortunately, fears have a way of becoming uncontrollable beasts. They can grow to terrible proportions and assume lives of their own. They even can come to *control* our personalities.

So what separates a normal and natural desire to avoid being shot by a handgun, from a case of ballistophobia? (fear of bullets) The difference is, the ballistophobiac is consumed by an irrational fear that he'll be killed by a bullet. His ability to move about freely in public places is crippled by an overwhelming anxiety that one day a stranger will emerge from a crowd and shoot him to death.

Granted, this is an extreme phobia. But don't many of us allow fear to hinder our daily activities in one way or another? Let's return for a moment to one of the "normal" fears we looked at earlier. I once knew a man who was so worried about the state of his financial resources, that he spent *hours* every week figuring and refiguring budgets for his family. He'd list his income, then record known expenses, projected expenses, and calculated expenses. From this information, he'd devise elaborate plans to ensure he'd have enough money left at the end of the month (or "financial time frame," as he called it) to pay his bills.

This fellow's preoccupation with budgets went far beyond a normal desire to be a good steward of his resources. In actuality, he was allowing the fear of a lack of resources to grip and manipulate his life.

What does all this mean? From a spiritual perspective, I'm convinced that fear often is a result of our not trusting God to take care of our needs. Naturally, "worrying" whether your favorite team is going to make it to the playoffs wouldn't fall into this category; all fears are *not* necessarily spiritually based. But when we allow fears to significantly determine the course of our behavior, in many instances, it's because we're doubting God's promise that He "will meet all [our] needs according to His glorious riches in Christ Jesus" (Phil. 4:19). If we truly believed that we did not have to be "anxious about anything" (Phil. 4:6), we wouldn't need to harbor fears about resources, abilities, or the unknown.

Therefore, at its root, fear often can be classified as a spiritual problem. Scripture repeatedly supports this interpretation. As Paul points out:

God hath not given us the spirit of fear (2 Tim. 1:7, KJV).

For you have not received a spirit of slavery leading to fear (Rom. 8:15, NASB).

The use of the word *spirit* in these verses is significant in that it points to the origin of fear. Fear is born in our souls— and from there it grows.

When Fear Comes Calling

Have you ever watched a scary movie, one replete with monsters and ghouls? Do you remember the fear you felt as you watched the hero or heroine unknowingly walk into the very room where some Frankensteinian creature lurked? At that moment, do you also remember your palms getting a bit more moist, your heart pounding just a little stronger, your mouth getting a tad drier?

All these sensations were mild physical reactions to a mild exposure to fear. Obviously, a case of sweaty palms posed no grave physical problems for you; this reaction was proportionate to the amount of fear you felt—which, in essence, was small and nonthreatening.

But what would happen to your body if worry, fear, or anxiety assumed larger proportions in your life? What if that fear hounded you for months on end? What if you were unable to shake "the spirit of fear"? Your physical reaction to fear would increase. And if your fear was the result of a lack of trust in God, it would be possible to medically document yet another link between the state of your spiritual health and that of your physical health.

If we're walking in a trust relationship with God, if we're putting our "trust in Him" (Heb. 2:13) to meet our every need, fear will not be able to lodge itself in our spirits. But if fear *is* calling the shots in our lives, we ought not be surprised when we find a host of physical maladies befalling us.

Some Case Studies in Fear

Today, the J.C. Penney department store chain is among the

most profitable in the nation. Even after the Crash of '29, Penney's continued to do a solid business. But few people know that during the dark days of the Depression, this chain's founder, James C. Penney, was troubled by a number of unwise personal commitments he had made. In fact, he so worried about his ability to honor these commitments that he often was unable to sleep. Eventually, his body reacted to this persistent fear in a more debilitating way: He developed *herpes zoster*—in his case, an anxiety-induced viral inflammation of the sensory ganglia of the spinal and cranial nerves. More popularly known as shingles, this illness produces painful skin eruptions. Penney's illness was the direct result of excessive fear and worry.

Fear also can lead to tension headaches. By clenching your fist for several minutes, you can easily demonstrate how tightened muscles produce pain. When someone is suffering from chronic anxieties or fears, his or her neck muscles similarly tighten. The result is a particularly painful headache.

In his classic work, *The Aeneid*, the Roman poet Vergil wrote:

> I was stupefied with fear; my hair stood on end and
> my voice stuck in my throat.

Vergil has accurately described two additional effects of fear. When our bodies are subjected to anxiety, our brains send lightening-quick messages of alarm to all parts of our bodies. Our hearts beat faster, our blood pressure rises, and our breathing accelerates. Another manifestation of this alarm reaction is for our hair follicles to tighten, which literally causes our hair to stand on end—just as Vergil observed!

As for the poet's voice "sticking in his throat," the body's fear-engendered alarm reaction also affects the secretion of our salivary glands. It indeed feels as though your voice is stuck in your throat when your mouth is dry. Perhaps that's why a glass of water is placed on the rostrum next to a nervous speaker—to compensate for fear's effect on the salivary juices.

A final illustration of the physical ramifications of fear should prove particularly interesting. Over the course of a few tragic months, Heather's teenage daughter had run away from home and her husband had left her. In addition to this grief, Heather now was worrying about her future. How was she going to manage on her own, how would she pay the bills, where would she find a job?

"My stomach tightens up and burns with pain," she told me, describing her symptoms. "These pangs feel almost as bad as when I was giving birth to my daughter. And at night, I'm so gripped by my awful fears, I just lie awake, trembling. I used to look forward to sleep—but now, I dread the nighttime."

The stomach and digestive tract are commonly affected by the type of extreme anxiety Heather was experiencing. Sleeplessness also is a standard symptom of excessive worry, as adrenalin released during such times prevents the body from relaxing. What was most interesting about Heather's case, however, was how it mirrored God's own description of the physical effects of fear. When she described her symptoms, I knew I'd heard the same words before—though not from another patient.

In the Book of Isaiah, the prophet describes the bodily reactions of a person consumed by fear. Isaiah's symptomology paralleled Heather's with amazing accuracy:

> At this my body is racked with pain, pangs seize me, like those of a woman in labor. . . . My heart falters, fear makes me tremble; the twilight I longed for has become a horror to me (Isa. 21:3-4).

As I read this verse, I was astonished at how closely my patient's condition reflected the words of Isaiah. But just as suddenly, my amazement passed. I realized I really had no reason to be surprised by this finding. After all, if fear can produce physical ailments, why shouldn't a similarity exist between the symptoms of anxious, worried people—even if the events which precipitated those fears occurred thousands of years apart?

God's Prescription for Fear

When last we saw J.C. Penney, he was suffering from painful skin eruptions. At one point during his illness, Penney became so overwhelmed by his fears and anxieties that he was convinced he actually was going to die. He even wrote farewell letters to his family, so sure was he that he would not live another day.

The next morning, however, Penney was still alive. In fact, he awoke to the sound of singing in the hospital chapel. He even recognized the name of the song; it was "God Will Take Care of You." As Penney later recalled:

> Suddenly, something happened. I can't explain it. I can only call it a miracle. I felt as if I had been instantly lifted out of the darkness of a dungeon into warm, brilliant sunlight. I felt as if I had been transported from hell to paradise. I felt the power of God as I had never felt it before. . . . I knew that God with His love was there to help me. From that day to this, my life has been free from worry (cited in Dale Carnegie, *How to Stop Worrying and Start Living,* Simon and Schuster, pp. 253-254).

The key to Penney's amazing recovery can be summarized in one word: faith. He realized that God's grace was sufficient to overcome his fears (2 Cor. 12:9), and so he placed his trust in God. By surrendering his fears to the One who was wholly adequate to deal with them, Penney's physical health drastically improved.

The Faith Factor

Many of us are well acquainted with the discussion of faith found in Hebrews 11. In this passage, faith is defined as "being sure of what we hope for and certain of what we do not see" (11:1). To this foundational understanding of faith, we can add several other characteristics.

Faith also has been defined as the leaning of our entire personality on God in absolute trust and confidence. Since God is powerful, wise, and good, we can place our trust in Him; it is this assurance that sustains us against fear, anxiety, and worry.

This particular understanding of faith carries with it certain implications. First, it means that we must be willing to give God total and absolute ownership of our lives. If He alone can supply all our needs, He alone is worthy of our unquestioning obedience, wholehearted service, and complete trust. By recognizing that God is greater than our fears, we can experience the Lord's presence, promises, protection, power, and provision.

Second, by appropriating God's prescription for fear, we can survive even the most anxious of moments—and no moment seems more anxious than the one in which we're faced with a crisis, and God seems oddly silent.

For weeks, Larry had been waiting to hear whether he'd been accepted for a job with a prestigious public relations firm. He knew he had the right qualifications for the position and that the firm was interested in him. But his interviewer had told him the firm was obliged to speak with several other candidates before making a decision.

Larry prayed constantly about the outcome of this matter. If it wasn't God's will for him to have this job, that would be fine—or so Larry tried to convince himself. In truth, Larry was becoming desperately anxious about this situation. During the course of his job search, bills continued to pour in, oblivious to his unemployed status. Larry had been unable to pay many of them, and now a number of creditors had threatened to send his accounts to a collection agency.

Where, Larry wondered, was God in all this? Intellectually, he *knew* that Jesus promised that all who trusted in Him would never be in need (Matt. 6:25-34). Still, God seemed strangely silent. When he prayed, Larry could not bring himself to do so in faith; and so he felt none of the assurance he usually experienced in his walk with God. All he had to show for his anxiety was a mounting pile of bills and a nasty tension headache.

The moral of this story is a simple one—one that doesn't even have anything to do with whether Larry got the job (though he did). The point is, we don't need to *feel* God's assurance to have faith in Him. Faith is a *fact,* not an emotional disposition. Had Larry known enough to take God's prescription for fear and anxiety, he'd have realized that faith can overcome the most insidious fear—even at times when God *does* seem distant.

Faith Applied

At the outset of this chapter, I mentioned three of man's more commonly experienced fears: fears over resources, abilities, and the unknown. However, we can quickly see that by applying God's prescription for fear—faith—each of these areas of concern can be triumphed over. Our spiritual health can be improved and we can avoid the debilitating physical effects of anxiety.

When we apply faith to our anxieties over resources, for example, we can confidently claim with Paul:

> And my God will meet all your needs according to
> His glorious riches in Christ Jesus (Phil. 4:19).

Did you hear that? God supplies *all* our needs—including our need for resources. This was a lesson I learned with striking clarity during my first year at college. I had been in school only three months when my father, who had just returned from medical work in China a year before, suffered a severe heart attack. The attack left him so weak, in fact, that he was unable to work for close to a year; as a result, the source of my tuition money gradually dried up. I seriously feared I'd lack the resources to finish school.

At times, things became particularly desperate. On one occasion, I found myself with nothing to eat. I had devoured the last of a few cornflakes for breakfast and prayed in faith that God would supply lunch and supper—though frankly, I really didn't have a clue as to where the food would come from.

When I went to my college mailbox that day, I found a single envelope waiting for me. Opening it, I discovered a note from the Chemistry Department. It read:

> Because you haven't broken your quota of glass-
> ware in your chemistry lab classes this semester,
> we are giving you a $10 refund.

I couldn't believe it! If my professors had polled the students who worked around me at my laboratory desk, I'm sure they'd have gotten an entirely different impression about how much glassware I'd shattered. But I was not about to look a gift horse in the mouth. More importantly, I was not about to question God's faithfulness. In a moment of worry over resources, I had turned to God and taken His prescription for my condition; He had supplied the much-needed grocery money and groceries. Late that same afternoon an elderly friend arrived at our front porch with a large bag of vegetables from her garden. She had walked twelve blocks to bring them. They arrived in time for the evening meal. Philippians 4:19 proved itself trustworthy again!

Elsewhere in Philippians Paul explains that faith can overcome yet another fear—our fear over our abilities:

> He who began a good work in you will carry it on
> to completion until the day of Christ Jesus (Phil.
> 1:6).

How often have you felt that God had a special plan for your life, but you were afraid you lacked the ability to fulfill that plan? It's reported that the great British preacher, George Whitefield, once suffered from a noticeable stutter. What if Whitefield had given in to the fear that God could never use him as a tool for the kingdom because of his impediment? Whole chapters in the history of British and American Christianity would never have been written! It's clear that Whitefield must have drawn on the richness of God's faithfulness to defeat the demon of fear. God's provision overcame Whitefield's worries about his ability to serve the Lord.

Finally, we can see how the prescription of faith can be applied to our fear of the unknown. First, let's consider two promises:

> You will keep in perfect peace him whose mind is steadfast, because he trusts in You (Isa. 26:3).

> Seek first His kingdom and His righteousness, and all these things will be given to you as well. Therefore do not worry about tomorrow (Matt. 6:33-34).

These are familiar verses to many people. But their familiarity should not dilute or diminish their impact on our lives. Even as you read those words, your life may be filled with a number of uncertainties: Should I accept a new job offer? Should I take a second mortgage on the house? Should I attend this or that college? All of these uncertainties—and many more—can be sources of anxiety. If allowed to run unchecked, they can lead to ulcers, arthritis, or even cancer (Michael Fauman, "The Central Nervous System and the Immune System," *Biological Psychiatry,* vol. 17, no. 12, 1982, p. 1459).

But the man or woman whose "mind is steadfast" knows that worrying over these concerns will accomplish nothing.

In the spiritual realm, the person who fears tomorrow, who fears what he neither can see nor control, is not exercising full trust in God. He is doubting the truth of every verse we've considered in this chapter. He is doubting "Him who is able to do immeasurably more than all we ask or imagine, according to His power" (Eph. 3:20).

As a physician, if I've heard that a number of respected medical professionals are strongly endorsing a cure for a particular illness, I'll give serious attention to it. I'll critically examine the claims being made and if I'm convinced that the medication or therapy achieves the desired results, I'll recommend it to my patients.

Allow me to recommend an extremely effective and time-tested antidote to fear and worry. Permit me to prescribe a treatment that can eliminate the spiritual and physical ravages of anxiety.

Introducing: Faith—the only prescription you and your family will ever need for the headaches, jitters, and upset stomachs caused by nagging, oppressive fear. Try it today. You'll be glad you did!

Chapter Five
The Place of Possessions

By the time he was thirty-three, John D. Rockefeller, Sr. already had made his first million dollars. By age forty-three, he controlled and operated what was then the largest corporation in the world—the Standard Oil Company. On his fifty-third birthday, he easily was the richest man on earth—and its only billionaire.

However, Rockefeller's relentless pursuit of money came at a terribly high cost. By consecrating his every waking moment to work, his health had badly deteriorated. He eventually developed alopecia, a condition in which the victim not only loses the hair from his head, but that from his eyelashes and eyebrows as well. His anxiety over his business ventures also severely affected his stomach. Imagine the irony of his situation: Rockefeller's weekly income was over $1 million, but his digestion was so poor he could eat only crackers and milk.

For much of his life, the American writer F. Scott Fitzgerald also was incessantly preoccupied with making money and living an extravagant life. Many of his biographers point out how he desperately wanted to be rich; yet whenever his writing *did* bring in money, he inevitably wasted it in ways that proved hazardous to his health. As A. Scott Berg notes:

[Fitzgerald] was again drinking too much. Later he wrote in his ledger that 1923 was a "comfortable but dangerous and deteriorating year." A few stories, a motion picture option, and various advances brought him almost $30,000 in 1923, $5,000 more than he had earned the year before. But after months of careless living, Fitzgerald admitted . . . he had spent himself into a "terrible mess" (*Max Perkins,* Dutton, p. 49).

After a lifetime of pursuing material wealth—and just as often losing what he had gained—Fitzgerald became an alcoholic and died of a heart attack at the relatively young age of forty-four.

John D. Rockefeller. F. Scott Fitzgerald. What did these two men have in common? Both were consumed by a desire to amass financial wealth and to achieve monetary success. Quite simply, both men were greedy.

It's worth noting that Rockefeller and Fitzgerald shared at least one other characteristic: Their inordinate desire for money was a prime cause of their health problems.

Unfortunately, their fates are far from unique. In a day and age when society touts the joys of materialism, increasing numbers of men and women are buying into the notion that monetary advancement is the *summum bonum*—the ultimate good—of human existence. But in the process of gaining more, more, more, they're losing their health.

So what exactly is the source of this compulsion? Why are so many people convinced that making enough money to live comfortably just isn't good enough? Why do they believe that extravagant wealth is so attractive? In short, why are people so greedy?

The Spiritual Roots of Greed

At its source, greed—that quality of "excessive or reprehensible acquisitiveness," as Webster puts it—is rooted in man's sinful nature. When Adam decided to follow his way rather than God's, he implicitly decided that certain *things* could bring him happiness. Having that fruit, for example, apparently seemed a lot more attractive than following God's instructions. And I think most of us would agree that Adam's desire to find happiness in "things" has been passed down to men of all generations. When this desire supercedes and overrules our desire to obey God, greed is born.

God, however, consistently has decried any attitude or desire which places material possessions over a devotion to Him. Scripture repeatedly exposes the greedy person for the sinful and unattractive individual he is:

> Ephraim boasts, "I am very rich; I have become wealthy. With all my wealth they will not find in me any iniquity or sin" (Hosea 12:8).

> A greedy man brings trouble to his family (Prov. 15:27).

> They are dogs with mighty appetites; they never have enough (Isa. 56:11).

> Men . . . who have been robbed of the truth and who think that godliness is a means to financial gain (1 Tim. 6:5).

Similarly, Luke notes that Judas "consented" to receiving money for his betrayal of Christ (Luke 22:6). Yet it is Paul who makes what is perhaps the most familiar observation concerning money and its potentially devastating influence:

> People who want to get rich fall into temptation and a trap and into many foolish and harmful desires that plunge men into ruin and destruction. For the love of money is a root of all kinds of evil (1 Tim. 6:9-10).

The apostle has driven home two very important points. First, he has confirmed the fact that "a love" of money, or greed, is intrinsically sinful. In his first letter to Timothy, in fact, Paul points out that a church leader must not be "a lover of money" (3:3). Please understand: Money, in and of itself, is not sinful. Jesus Himself, cited many acceptable uses for legal tender (Luke 12:33; Matt. 5:3; 19:21). Paul's argument, however, is that when a desire for money adversely affects our relationship with God, our family, or others, it probably has become a sinful desire. More on this subject in just a bit.

Now, to get back to the second point Paul is making in this passage. By noting that the desire to "get rich" leads to "harmful" consequences, it seems evident that the apostle was thinking of the spiritual harm caused by greed, such as our reduced appreciation of spiritual values. Yet it also is conceivable that he was referring to the *physical* consequences of greed or covetousness. Once again, it's possible to illustrate that a spiritual problem—greed—can have an effect on our physical health.

The Physical Effects of Greed

So far, we've seen how greed caused two men to suffer from alopecia and alcoholism. However, there are a number of other possible physical consequences of overwhelming materialistic urges.

Obviously, greed—in itself—does not *directly* have physical manifestations. However, the emotional states produced by concern, anxiety, or overwork associated with a person's compulsion to have money, *do* have clear physical ramifications. For example, in Rockefeller's case, the tycoon's intense, concentrated effort to pursue money led him to barter away his health.

Dean contacted my answering service late one weekday night. He said he needed to see me immediately. Shortly thereafter, I met him in the hospital emergency room, where I learned he had been vomiting and suffering from painful abdominal cramps, diarrhea, and headaches for nearly a week.

As I asked him a series of routine questions about his recent dietary habits, it became increasingly clear that Dean's problems were not a result of what he had been eating; rather, his ailment was the result of what had been eating *him.*

Dean was a loan officer with one of the largest banks in the area. He'd been with this institution for nearly three years and had risen quickly within it. With each promotion, of course, he received a raise that was both substantial and commensurate with his new responsibilities. As a result of his advancement, he'd been able to make a down payment on an attractive townhouse and purchase a neat little sports car.

It was a rosy picture of success—until Dean learned through the bank's grapevine that he'd risen as far in the organization as he could expect to go. His superiors felt Dean knew his job *so* well, they couldn't afford to move him out of his present position. With this freeze in his advancement, subsequent raises would be quite a bit smaller than he had become accustomed to.

Dean clearly was making enough money to meet his present financial obligations. But that wasn't enough—at least as far as he was concerned. He *liked* the raises he was getting—he almost *craved* them—and he wanted *more.*

After receiving this dread news, his body had reacted to it quickly. What exactly had happened? Basically, Dean's very strong interest in money—and the short-circuiting of prospects to satisfy that interest—had set off a tempest in his body's emotional center. Nerve impulses from this center rapidly initiated and perpetuated his vomiting and severe cramps. These same impulses opened up the blood vessels in his face and neck; the increased amount of blood which flowed into his skull led to his headaches and exacerbated his vomiting.

Another case study futher illustrates the physical shortcomings of greed. Following the series of successful U. S.

moon landings in the early 1970s, Congress began curtailing further funds for the manned space program. As a result, a number of scientists and other highly skilled personnel were released from the program. It soon became apparent that they would find little opportunity to use their specialized skills elsewhere; after all, the United States only had one space program. But because their employment had been extremely lucrative, many of the men and women who worked for NASA had adopted extremely expensive life-styles; now, with their prospects for employment minimal, a number of these employees experienced severe physical reactions.

Obviously, not all of these individuals were money-mongers. Some were simply average people with extraordinary financial problems. But a number of these people had become tremendously attracted to the financial advances which their careers had produced. The frustration of their greed eventually led to a rash of fatal and near-fatal heart attacks among this group of ex-space personnel.

Dr. Rudolph Oehm reports that post-mortem examinations performed on these persons uncovered a most unusual phenomenon. Rather than finding typical curvy fibers upon microscopic examination of their heart muscles, he found unusual "contraction bands." Since that time, these "bands" have been correlated with stress and a high secretion of certain body hormones, such as adrenalin and noradrenalin (*The Joy of Good Health,* Harvest House, pp. 69-70). The source of their stress, of course, was related to money.

God's Prescription for Greed

Once again, it's abundantly clear that attitudes and behaviors which distance us from God can be hazardous to our health. But God has provided a remedy for the ills generated by selfishness and greed.

Of course, some prescriptions are harder to take than others. I know that some of my patients have reacted poorly to certain medications I've prescribed for them. A liquid medication may taste terrible or a pill may have a color quality that looks hideous; on rare occasions, such medication has even induced nausea in a patient who wasn't previously nauseous. While I don't necessarily subscribe to the old adage, "if it doesn't taste bad, it's not good for you," I realize that a prescription that's truly good for someone sometimes is literally "hard to swallow."

So it is with God's prescription for greed. Covetousness, worldliness, fortune-hunting, materialism. Whatever label you attach to it, greed is a serious spiritual illness. As such, it calls for serious treatment. Scripture seems to indicate a two-part prescription for this particular sickness of the soul.

First, the greedy individual must learn to break his addiction to money; if need be, he must even be willing to relinquish some of his possessions. Secondly, he must share what he has with others.

Now do you see why this is a difficult treatment to accept? Perhaps it would be best, then, to examine this prescription in light of scriptural teaching, and then consider specific, real-life examples of people who have appropriated God's remedy in this area.

Relinquishing Possessions

The Gospel of Luke contains two excellent case studies on the subject of greed. In one, we see a man who takes God's prescription and discovers the results of obedience. In the other, Luke tells of a man who is offered the same prescription, but finds it too bitter to swallow.

The first case study involves the tax collector, Zaccheus. Luke makes note of the fact that Zaccheus was wealthy (19:2), perhaps to emphasize the importance which money played in his life. Luke also mentions that Jesus visited Zaccheus' home. Unfortunately, Luke does *not* record the conversation that took place between these two men. But meeting Jesus face-to-face must have had a tremendous impact on Zaccheus, for he makes a startling statement:

> Look, Lord! Here and now I give half of my posses-
> sions to the poor, and if I have cheated anybody
> out of anything, I will pay back four times the
> amount (Luke 19:8).

Can you imagine it? Zaccheus not only was a tax collector,
he was a *chief* collector (19:2). He could not have risen to
this position of authority without a great deal of hard work—
and treachery. (If you think the Internal Revenue Service is
rough on taxpayers, you should have lived in Jericho in A.D.
32. Forget about being called in for an audit; a failure to pay
certain taxes there was punishable by *death.*) Yet now this
chief tax collector was offering to give away a full 50 percent
of his possessions! And to those whom he had cheated—who
surely were legion—he was repaying with 400 percent interest attached!

Obviously, Zaccheus saw something in Christ that he knew
money could never buy: peace, serenity, a sense of walking
in God's favor. Perhaps this tax collector also realized that far
from being able to *purchase* such attributes, money might
actually be a *hindrance* to obtaining them. Zacchaeus realized that his greed was, in essence, separating him from God.
So Zaccheus relinquished what he had in order to gain
something of even greater value—a relationship with the
living God. Jesus expressed the very principle that motivated
Zaccheus' action in His Parable of the Pearl:

> Again, the kingdom of heaven is like a merchant
> looking for fine pearls. When he found one of great
> value, he went away and sold everything he had
> and bought it (Matt. 13:45-46).

The result of Zaccheus' obedience? "Today," the Lord said,
"salvation has come to this house" (Luke 19:9). Zaccheus took God's prescription for greed, gave up his

possessions, and was blessed in return.

Luke also makes note of another instance in which Jesus prescribed this same remedy for greed—relinquishing possessions. Only in this case, the prescription was rejected:

> A certain ruler asked Him, "Good Teacher, what must I do to inherit eternal life?"
>
> "Why do you call Me good?" Jesus answered. "No one is good—except God alone. You know the commandments: 'Do not commit adultery, do not murder, do not steal, do not give false testimony, honor your father and mother.' "
>
> "All these I have kept since I was a boy," he said.
>
> When Jesus heard this, He said to him, "You still lack one thing. Sell everything you have and give to the poor, and you will have treasure in heaven. Then come, follow Me."
>
> When he heard this, he became very sad, because he was a man of great wealth (Luke 18:18-23).

In commenting on Jesus' instruction to the young ruler, Bible commentators Walvoord and Zuck observe:

> The ruler was not prepared to take that step. The ruler was more attached to his wealth than to the idea of obtaining "eternal life" which he had so nobly asked about at the beginning of his conversation with the Lord. . . . Riches often cloud a person's thinking about what is truly important in life (*The Bible Knowledge Commentary,* Victor Books, pp. 250-251).

What more is there to say? Jesus offered the young ruler God's prescription for greed, and he refused it. Contrast the ruler's response to this prescription with Zaccheus' the ruler "became very sad," while Zaccheus responded to the Lord's instruction and was saved.

A willingness to relinquish possessions. It seems like a terribly difficult thing to do. And what exactly does this instruction mean for us in terms of our daily lives? If I'm feeling greedy, does that mean I should sell my house and car and take to wearing sackcloth?

This is, of course, a difficult matter—and one for which there are no pat answers. However, I believe that if a person is serious about maintaining his or her spiritual health, and greed is threatening it, one principle should be followed. Specifically, identify the thing or things about which you're feeling covetous and renounce them. For example, if you find yourself with an overwhelming desire to constantly increase the size of your stereo system, it might not be a bad idea just to get rid of the thing. That's right. Just give it up. In a nutshell, that stereo system has become an idol to you; it's attracting your attention and drawing your devotion away from God. Remember: We are to have no other gods but Him (Ex. 20:3). Anything that threatens this relationship must be dealt with.

If after doing without your stereo for awhile you find you've regained a proper understanding of the relation between God and mammon, you may be ready to buy another one. But be careful! If we don't willingly relinquish possessions that hinder our spiritual health, God may teach us a lesson the hard way! *He'll* take our possessions from us.

As I mentioned earlier, the first years of my life were spent in China. However, those years just happened to coincide with the tumultuous pre- and post- Second World War era—not exactly the time and place to experience a normal childhood. In 1935, our family was forced to flee from Communist forces that were sweeping China during an abortive revolution. In 1940, three years after the Japanese Army invaded China, we again needed to run for our lives. In 1949, we were evacuated from Shanghai two weeks before the Red Army finally seized that city.

A common thread ran through all of these experiences. In

each, the particular invading army got all of our furnishings and all of the goods inside our house. When we left Ethiopia in 1975, the result was similar. Most of our medical equipment and personal belongings had to be left behind.

But you see, having had our earthly possessions removed from us four times—without the bother and fuss of a garage sale—reinforced a very important lesson:

> You were actually joyful when all you owned was taken from you, knowing that better things were awaiting you in heaven, things that would be yours forever (Heb. 10:34, TLB).

Of course, having one's possessions forcibly taken away is a bit different than voluntarily *giving* them away. And I don't think God sent these experiences into my life because my family was covetous. But seeing that God never forsook me or my family during those difficult times simply strengthened my belief that the "cheerful giver" described in 2 Corinthians will be the recipient of God's grace as well. When we realize that all good things come from God, we can freely relinquish what we own. We know that He *will* care for us (Matt. 6:33).

Giving to Others

Obviously, if we're going to give of our possessions as we renounce greediness, our giving must be directed toward real people with real needs. This fact was alluded to earlier, when we saw, for example, how Zaccheus gave his money to those whom he had swindled.

Scripture points out the relationship between relinquishing possessions and giving to those who have needs:

> The righteous give without sparing (Prov. 21:26).

> All the believers were one in heart and mind. No one claimed that any of his possessions was his

own, but they shared everything they had. . . .
There were no needy persons among them. For
from time to time those who owned lands or
houses sold them, brought the money from the
sales, and put it at the apostles' feet, and it was
distributed to anyone as he had need (Acts
4:32, 34-35).

On the first day of every week, each one of you
should set aside a sum of money in keeping with
his income, saving it up, so that when I come no
collections will have to be made (1 Cor. 16:2).

Out of the most severe trial, their overflowing joy
and their extreme poverty welled up in rich generosity. For I testify that they gave as much as they
were able, and even beyond their ability (2 Cor.
8:2-3).

Can you imagine how powerful our faith would become if
we adopted this same attitude today? What would the world
think if the body of Christ freely gave of its possessions to
help the needy? I can only assume the results would be the
same as in the days of the early church: "And the Lord added
to their number daily those who were being saved" (Acts
2:47). That would be just one of the consequences of a
widespread renunciation of selfishness and greed.

But the blessing would not stop there. As the theme of this
book suggests, our physical health also would benefit from a
turning away from covetousness. If you recall, at the beginning of this chapter, we saw how greed had ravaged the
physical frame of John D. Rockefeller, Sr. But in *None of
These Diseases,* S.I. McMillen tells of the drastic improvement in Rockefeller's health once he appropriated the spiritual principles outlined in this chapter:

For the first time in his life he recognized that

money was not a commodity to be hoarded but something to be shared for the benefit of others. . . . He established the Rockefeller Foundation so that some of his fortune could be channeled to needed areas. . . . His money sparked the research that saved and is still saving millions of people from untimely deaths from malaria, tuberculosis, diphtheria, and many other diseases. . . . When he began to think *outwardly* toward the needs of others, a miracle occurred. He began to sleep, to eat normally, and to enjoy life in general. He who had been repulsive and lifeless now teemed with vibrancy and activity. . . . When Rockefeller was fifty-three, it certainly appeared that he would never celebrate another birthday, but he started to practice one of God's eternal laws, and he reaped its promised benefits: "Give, and it shall be given unto you; good measure, pressed down, shaken together, running over, shall they give into your bosom." He proved the value of this promise for he lived not only until his fifty-fourth and fifty-fifth birthdays, but he experienced "the good measure . . . running over"—he lived until he was ninety-eight years old (Revell, p. 129).

While Rockefeller's recovery may seem a "miracle" to some, I believe it was the result of his simple recognition that money could not bring him happiness. It certainly had not brought him physical health. Only when he took God's prescription for greed was his physical strength restored.

When we take this same prescription today, we can begin a new life of health and satisfaction under the care of the Master Physician.

Chapter Six
Take Seven Times Daily

Moses had a lot of firsthand experience dealing with discontented, complaining, cynical people. Imagine what he was up against when the newly liberated nation of Israel found itself trapped by the Red Sea. Pharaoh's chariots were fast approaching and certain slaughter seemed imminent. What did the Israelites do? Did they band together behind Moses? Support him with an overwhelming vote of confidence? Start a fervent prayer meeting?

No way! They began whining!

"Was it because there were no graves in Egypt that you brought us to the desert to die?" they sniveled. "It would have been better for us to serve the Egyptians than to die in the desert!" (Ex. 14:11-12) Picture it: 600,000 men—with their wives and families—all complaining. Just what Moses needed.

Yet we know that God delivered Israel from this seemingly helpless situation. You'd think that after having seen a sea parted, God's chosen people would've been much less likely to gripe about their circumstances the next time trouble arose. But, alas, Moses repeatedly discovered that Israel's capacity for complaining knew few bounds.

On any number of occasions, he heard them grumping

about water (Ex. 15:24; 17:2), food (Ex. 16:3), and his leadership abilities (Num. 12:2; 14:2). The worst part of it was poor Moses had to put up with this complaining for forty years!

Israel's problem, as the Lord once pointed out to Moses, was essentially a spiritual one (Deut. 9:13). Their incessant complaining reflected their failure to see that God was in control of each and every situation they confronted.

We would do well to take note of this fact in our own lives. And indeed we shall, as we focus on the spiritual and physical hazards of complaining.

Why Do We Complain?

We don't like commands. One reason we complain is because we don't like to be told what to do. This principle operates on both a spiritual and a temporal level.

Let's return to our friends in the Sinai Desert for a moment. I can well imagine that one ingredient which contributed to the Israelites' penchant for grousing was that they didn't like God's commands for them. When Moses led them out of Egypt, the Children of Israel probably figured the Lord was going to send them, via the quickest route, to the nearest spot of paradise. Maybe some place that was rich and lush, like the fertile banks of the Tigris. A man could set himself up real well there.

When instead, God ordered them into the barren desert, more than a few hopes were shattered—and more than a few necks stiffened. God's commands clearly flew in the face of what the nation of Israel had envisioned for itself.

This story illustrates the problem we often have with receiving and obeying divine commands. Many of us also tend to exhibit this attitude when we're asked to obey seemingly arbitrary commands from other *humans.* If you've ever heard someone say, "Nobody tells me what to do," "I'm my own boss," or "I don't take orders," you understand what I mean. Humans are rugged individualists—both by disposition and tradition—and we have a hard time acquiescing to commands or orders which we believe threaten, inhibit, or destroy our self-autonomy. When faced with such commands, we complain about them.

We don't like to be mismanaged. It's also possible to identify another source of complaining that applies both to our relationship with God and men.

Among a list of current best-selling books are a number that deal with how to effectively *manage* your life: *Mary Kay on People Management, Putting the One-Minute Manager to Work, The One-Minute Salesperson.* The popularity of these books attests to the fact that most of us want to feel that we're truly in control of our lives. Of course, if we feel that someone is *mis*managing us—depriving us of our control and steering us down the wrong path—we'll complain.

Don't we also do this with God? There have been times in my life when I've felt as though He's been mismanaging me. In 1976, I was working as a surgeon at the Central DuPage Hospital in Winfield, Illinois. While I was grateful for this job, inwardly I had a burning desire to return to Ethiopia and to my work at a mission hospital in Soddo. Yet try as I might to arrange things for my return there, the Lord constantly seemed to be constructing barriers to the fulfillment of my plans: He increased my responsibilities at the hospital, and with various Christian organizations in the area. He was making it impossible for me to return to Ethiopia.

At this point, some of you might be wondering why anyone in his right mind would want to abandon the luxury and affluence of an American medical practice to return to an African mission hospital. But that was just the point: I felt that I could do God a greater service in a country where medical care was years behind the current technology. So as I sat in my comfortable, suburban office, I couldn't help but feel that somehow, God was mismanaging my life, my career, and my service to Him. Why wouldn't He let me go back to Ethiopia? I spent quite a bit of time griping about this turn of events.

We don't believe God. Finally, in treating this question from a purely spiritual perspective, I believe a major reason we complain is because we don't believe God's promises. The psalmist, reflecting on Moses' problems in the wilderness, sheds some light on this idea:

> Then they despised the pleasant land; they did not
> believe His promise. They grumbled in their tents
> and did not obey the Lord (Ps. 106:24-25).

From the very beginning, God had promised Israel that He would be with them, lead them, and protect them (Ex. 6:6-8). In addition to these verbal assurances, His *actions* confirmed that His promises were not merely empty words. When manna and quail fell from the skies, when water gushed from the rock, when a codified system of Law was provided to guide Israel's religious and civil life—God's promises were validated entirely.

And yet, Israel complained. Why? Because in their spiritual immaturity, they failed to believe that God would continue to honor His word. Lest we be too harsh with these men and women, let us remember that all too often, we share their frailty. At various times in my life, God has miraculously spared me from shipwreck, drowning, Communist invasion, a full-scale ship's mutiny, diphtheria, and a host of other calamities. On more occasions than I can count, He's wondrously provided for my every need. Yet I still catch myself complaining about some little problem: My car won't start on a cold morning; a utility bill seems too high. But then I remember: I don't need to worry about such matters. And I certainly don't have to complain about them. God has *promised* He'll never leave me or forsake me (Heb. 13:5).

What Happens When We Complain?

It's been my experience that individuals who complain about other people, who gripe about their problems, or who moan over how misunderstood they are, tend to become cynical. The cynic, as Webster defines him, is "a faultfinding captious critic." He's someone who's so accustomed to seeing the negatives in life, that for him, life has *become* negative. Complaining is his trademark.

However, according to a recent study conducted by psychiatrists at the Duke University Medical Center, the cynical, complaining heart may be a very unhealthy one.

In the 1950s, cardiologists Meyer Friedman and Ray Rosenman discovered that individuals who were impatient, who walked and ate quickly, interrupted others, and complained constantly, were more likely to suffer heart problems than other individuals. Friedman and Rosenman labeled these caustic complainers, "Type A" personalities; their calmer counterparts were called "Type B's." Follow-up studies conducted at various research facilities supported these findings.

But now, Duke researcher Redford Williams believes that some components of Type A behavior are physically more damaging than others. In conjunction with psychologist Paul Costa of the National Institute on Aging, Williams believes he has isolated one such damaging component: cynicism.

Williams administered a section of the Minnesota Multiphasic Personality Inventory (MMPI) that measures hostility and cynicism to more than 1,500 patients being examined for artherosclerotic symptoms. Those with high levels of cynical, complaining behavior were 50 percent more likely to have clogged arteries than those who scored low. Since the MMPI has been used extensively since the 1950s, researchers were able to consult earlier test results and confirm Williams' finding. One study of 255 physicians who took the test 25 years earlier showed that those with high "cynicism" scores had 5 times the level of heart disease than those who scored below the median.

Further laboratory experiments have shown that Type A personalities also produce more of certain types of hormones in certain situations than do less discontented individuals. Since these hormones are believed to accelerate plaque buildup on artery walls—"hardening" of the arteries—those people who find a great deal to complain about in life may not find themselves experiencing it much longer.

Psalm 106 describes the utter sorrow and dejection of Israel in the wilderness.

> Many times [God] delivered them, but they were bent on rebellion and they wasted away in their sin. But He took note of their distress when He heard their cry; for their sake He remembered His covenant and out of His great love He relented. He caused them to be pitied by all who held them captive (Ps. 106:43-46).

God's Prescription for Complaining

Fortunately, we belong to a God who wants good things for us, who does not desire to see us trapped in cages of our own making. Fortunately, in Scripture, He has provided us with a blueprint for overcoming the spiritual and physical ravages of a complaining personality. To appropriate God's prescription for complaining and cynicism, we need to recognize certain fundamental truths.

God wants what's good and perfect for us. When we find ourselves in a situation where it seems our lives are being mismanaged, or in which we're commanded to do something that sounds ridiculous, there's an alternative to griping. We can realize that in all situations, God has a specific and special plan for our life. Regardless of how circumstances may *appear,* nothing can annihilate that plan; ultimately, all things *do* serve to further His will (Rom. 8:28). In many instances, a recognition of this fact can materially improve one's health.

Several passages from God's Word point to His sovereignty and goodness with regard to our personal situations.

In Genesis, we read how Joseph greeted his brothers, years after they sold him into slavery. If anyone was qualified to complain about having been mistreated, Joseph certainly would rank right up there. Yet consider his attitude:

> Don't be afraid. Am I in the place of God? You intended to harm me, but God intended it for good to accomplish what is now being done, the saving of many lives (Gen. 50:19-20).

It's not too difficult to picture the former inhabitants of Jerusalem believing that God had tragically mismanaged their lives when Nebuchadnezzar carried Israel into exile in Babylon. After all, how could they possibly serve Him in a foreign land? It's also easy to picture the complaining that must have raged in the Israelites' hearts as they considered their predicament.

However, during this very period in Israel's history, God spoke to His people through the Prophet Jeremiah. There's no reason for Israel to be cynical or discontent about their situation, for:

> "I know the plans I have for you," declares the Lord, "plans to prosper you and not to harm you, plans to give you hope and a future" (Jer. 29:11).

In his epistle, James writes:

> Blessed is the man who perseveres under trial, because when he has stood the test, he will receive the crown of life that God has promised to those who love Him (James 1:12).

With that kind of assurance in mind, I can trust God implicitly. When faced with an opportunity to doubt God's sovereignty over my life, I can rest peacefully in the knowledge that His throne "will last forever and ever" (Heb. 1:8).

We must learn to praise God. This morning, our house seemed quiet and still. You see, our children have followed

God's leading and now are serving Him in Africa. As I walked from room to room, reminiscing over years past, I paused for a moment in my daughter's bedroom. There, on her desk, was a small sign which read:

> A cheerful heart is good medicine, but a crushed spirit dries up the bones (Prov. 17:22).

I smiled as I thought of how well Carolyn practices the spirit of that verse, how well she manages to maintain her cheerfulness even when confronted with events she legitimately could complain about.

I then began to wonder about how she manages to perform this all-too-difficult feat. If only I could harness the secret of that cheerfulness and share it with my patients, I thought, a great deal of physical and spiritual suffering could be avoided. Suddenly, I remembered two verses from Psalms that answered my question.

"His praise will always be on my lips" (Ps. 34:1). "Seven times a day I praise you" (119:164). These verses are so important because they describe the *attitude* we should strive to maintain when we're tempted to complain. The words *always* in the first verse and *seven times a day* in the second underscore the importance of making praise a continuous part of our Christian experience.

My daughter is able to triumph over cynicism and discontent because she has learned the value of praise. Because she actively thanks God for all His many blessings, she simply doesn't have *time* to gripe about arbitrary orders or perceived attempts to mismanage her life.

I must admit, though, that I had to chuckle when I realized that part of God's remedy for complaining is to praise Him seven times a day. Perhaps it's because I'm a physician, but when I recalled that verse, I felt as though I was reading a prescription off a medicine bottle. You know what I mean: *Take three times a day, before meals, with liquid.*

But then I became somewhat concerned. If you've ever

noticed, few medical prescriptions call for a person to take a dosage *seven* times a day. Most patients simply would find such a request too inconvenient. That's why the pharmaceutical industry has been hard at work developing medications that need only to be taken once or twice a day. That way, doctors can be assured that their patients are receiving the proper amount of medication.

So what does all this have to do with my sudden concern? Well, I wondered whether many people might also find the prescription to praise the Lord "seven times a day" as burdensome as having to swallow a pill every few hours. After all, aren't most of us usually busy, darting here and there, shouldered with a ton of responsibilities? Certainly, we don't have time to take this spiritual prescription seven times a day!

As hard as it may seem, I'd like to encourage you to try this remedy exactly as God prescribed it. Unlike the pharmaceutical industry, the Almighty is not in the business of seeking streamlined methods to improve our spiritual and physical health. He has no pill to offer which, if popped once daily with water, will help us stop complaining. He's yet to develop a time-release capsule that will clear up our cynicism and lead to eighteen hours of uninterrupted cheerfulness.

God has, however, given us a prescription that's every bit as effective as these fanciful medications—even if it *does* take a bit of effort on our part to take it. If we're praising Him continuously, we'll discover just how difficult it is to keep on complaining. It's that simple. It's that challenging. It's that wonderful.

We need to dwell on God's characteristics. In 1966, I was finishing a stint as the chief of surgery for the U.S. Navy in Taiwan. After leaving this assignment, I had planned to go to Africa and begin surgical work in Ethiopia. However, my mission board informed me that before my family and I could depart for the Dark Continent, we first would have to spend a year in the United States, visiting churches. The point of this visitation work, of course, was to tell people exactly what we would be doing in Africa. Hopefully, they'd then provide the financial support we needed to underwrite our work there.

You can imagine my reaction to this news. I immediately complained that this request was unwise. A year spent traveling across the width and breadth of America would do little to improve my surgical skills. In fact, the longer I was away from an operating table, the more my skills would deteriorate. Once again, I thought, I was being mismanaged.

Well, to make a long story short, two weeks before I was to leave Taiwan, God provided all of our support for Africa. This truly was a blessing. I was able to keep right on operating as God kept right on supplying my needs.

The turning point in this mini-drama occurred, however, when I took a moment to *stop* complaining, and to *start* considering exactly what type of God I was serving. My God is holy, righteous, just, and faithful. He is omnipresent, omniscient, and omnipotent. His loving-kindness is eternal and unchangeable.

When I paused to fully appreciate these characteristics of the Most High—to really meditate on their meaning—I understood that I had no cause to complain. Oh, as a human creature with the gift of free will, I certainly could grumble and mumble if I *wanted* to. I also could let myself develop an ulcer or heart disease as a consequence.

I've realized afresh that my complaining must seem laughable in His eyes. If I really believe God possesses the attributes I've just named, I can trust Him in every circumstance. I don't need to complain about *anything*.

Do You Need to Change Your Name?

Hopefully, by now we've come to see that we have few legitimate excuses to complain. Discontent should not be an attitude which characterizes someone who knows and trusts Jesus Christ. Complaining should not be a part of our conduct. A story I heard my pastor tell illustrates this point.

After a successful military campaign, Alexander the Great was known to reward soldiers who performed bravely and to punish those who had demonstrated cowardice. On one occasion, while celebrating a victory with his generals, Alexander's guards dragged a young soldier before him. The man had been charged with deserting his post, and was now to receive Alexander's sentence.

The automatic penalty for such an offense usually was death. But for a reason known only to him, this time, Alexander hesitated. He looked down on the young soldier—who was trembling and prostrate before him—and asked a simple question.

"Soldier, what is your name?"

"Alexander," the young man whispered weakly.

"*What* is your name?" Alexander asked again, his voice rising in anger.

"Alexander," the soldier repeated, ashamedly.

In a flash, the great ruler was upon the man. He grabbed him by the front of his tunic and yanked him face-to-face.

"That's *my* name," Alexander roared. Then, in a suddenly soft—but harsh—tone, he continued:

"Soldier, you shall live. But from this day on, you either must change your *conduct,* or you must change your *name!*"

Alexander's point, of course, was that if the soldier was to share his name, he must behave in a way that was consistent with the ruler's reputation and character.

If we are to bear the name *Christian,* we too must demonstrate behavior that proves us worthy of that name. The person who spends his life complaining is hard pressed to accomplish that goal.

Chapter Seven
In the Storm

It was 1940. Though the Japanese Imperial Army had occupied China for the past three years, my parents had managed to continue their missionary work among the Chinese people. Yet as world tensions mounted, and war between Japan and the United States became increasingly likely, we received a message from the American Embassy in Beijing: The U.S. Government could no longer guarantee our protection if we remained in China. We would have to evacuate immediately.

Several days after that directive was issued, I found myself headed for San Francisco aboard the *S.S. Washington,* which was, at one-tenth of a mile long, one of the largest ships in the American fleet. But this would be no pleasure cruise.

For some time prior to our evacuation, many Americans living in occupied China had heard a persistent rumor: Japan was planning to launch a surprise attack against American ships *before* officially declaring war. The captain of the *Washington* had heard—and believed—this bit of information. As a result, he decided not to take any chances with his ship on this particular voyage home. He would employ evasive action.

The captain knew, for example, that it would take a Japanese submarine at least six minutes to aim and accurately fire its torpedoes at the *Washington.* Consequently, every six minutes during our trip, he put the ship through a series of sharp, disorienting turns.

It was our captain's second precautionary measure, though, that I remember best. Rather than taking a direct—and hence, potentially more dangerous—route between China and the United States, the skipper set a course that ran along Alaska's Aleutian Islands. Yet this area of the world was—and is—notorious for one thing: big storms. In the summer of 1940, I had an opportunity to observe the Aleutians' stormy reputation up close.

The waves of the storms we went through, as judged by the *Washington's* captain, approached eighty-five feet in height. A lesser ship surely would have been swamped—which is not to say that the *Washington* went unscathed. On the contrary, the ship rocked horrendously. People literally were hurled down corridors or steps as killer waves smacked our ship. The most graphic testimony to the storm's destructive power was the fact that when we reached San Francisco, more than 150 of the *Washington's* passengers had an arm or leg in a cast. Believe me, after it was over, we knew we'd been through a storm!

In the years since that experience, I've come to realize that violent storms are not confined solely to oceans or to tropical zones frequented by hurricanes. They often occur in our *lives.* I'm referring, of course, to those tempestuous, gut-wrenching, faith-trying times of life when it seems that a good part of the universe is falling atop us. We lose a job, our spouse dies, or a host of similar evils occur. And in many instances, we find that these storms can leave their marks on our physical health as well as our souls.

I believe it's possible, however, to handle the storms of our lives by examining them from a spiritual perspective. I'm convinced that the negative effects of such problem situations often could be avoided, or minimized, simply by being aware of a few biblical principles. But to deal effectively with our storms, we first must try to understand their various sources.

Where Do Storms Come From?

It takes two to tango. From a meteorological perspective, storms usually develop when two or more air masses collide and conflict with one another. Substitute the word *people* for the phrase *air masses,* and you've got a pretty fair idea of where a lot of our emotional storms originate. Quite simply, if we're experiencing difficulties with other individuals, and we handle these interpersonal conflicts in an unscriptural fashion, we're likely to experience an emotional storm.

Take Elise, for example. She works as a secretary in a large marketing company, and has been a Christian for nearly seven years. Unfortunately, Elise's immediate supervisor is a petty despot who enjoys lording his authority over Elise and her coworkers. The supervisor is pompous, short-tempered, and ill-mannered—all "perfect" ingredients to generate conflict with other more well-adjusted individuals.

On a number of occasions, Elise's supervisor has unfairly criticized her work or started false rumors about her. Regrettably, Elise has responded in kind to these actions. In an effort to "get back" at her boss, she's adopted the supervisor's own methods: slander and innuendo. By seeking an "eye for an eye," however, she's now locked in a hopeless, tormenting battle. Every day, Elise undergoes a war of wills with her supervisor—and she's getting increasingly frustrated and depressed in the process. She doesn't want to quit her job, but she doesn't know how to break out of this vicious circle without "losing face." Elise is caught in a storm.

Disobedience. Elise's personal storm was, of course, due largely to her boss' antagonizing nature. There are other types of storms, though, that are mostly *self*-produced. In these instances, the storm's source is primarily *spiritual.*

In an earlier chapter, we examined the spiritual ills that befell King David when he entered into his illicit relationship with Bathsheba. David's desires drove him to possess this woman. Nothing would stand in the way of his having her; he even planned Bathsheba's husband's death so he could marry her. But as the author of 2 Samuel tersely observes: "The thing David had done displeased the Lord" (2 Sam. 11:27).

Surely, from the moment he conceived it, David must have been aware that his course of action would anger God. He was well acquainted with the Law; adultery and murder both were expressly forbidden. And yet, by deliberately choosing his own will over God's, by disobeying the Lord's holy statutes, David had effectively plunged himself into a storm. A short time after David's marriage to Bathsheba, the Lord sent Nathan the prophet to expose the King's transgressions. And expose them he did!

At this point, David's storm began in earnest. He anguished over his sin. He acknowledged his wrongdoing, but was hounded by guilt and remorse over it. His own words describe the depth of the torment he was experiencing:

> For I know my transgressions, and my sin is always
> before me. Against You, You only, have I sinned
> and done what is evil in Your sight. . . . Surely I
> have been a sinner from birth, sinful from the time
> my mother conceived me (Ps. 51:3-5).

How many of us can identify with David's lament? How many of *our* storms arise when we willingly disobey God's revealed will for our lives?

Your enemy, Satan. "I can't believe it." His words sounded flat, hollow, almost disembodied. "Everything was going fine, just great. Now *this.*" He slowly shook his head. "Why did God let this happen?"

Harry was a church deacon, and his reaction to my telling him that he had cancer of the prostate was not unusual. Many Christians go through life in a seeming state of perpetual grace. Unlike Elise, they manage to cope with personality clashes in a spirit of Christian love. Unlike David, they are eager to obey God's direction for their lives. Then, suddenly, like the proverbial bolt out of the blue, a storm strikes. Cancer, unemployment, a family tragedy. Their world spins out of orbit. They don't know what to do next.

At such times, it's vital to remember a third source of storms. Sometimes, in His divine providence, God allows Satan to bring trials, tests, and storms into His children's lives. Of course, we know that the Lord, Himself, never tempts anyone (James 1:13). But He *does* allow an already-defeated devil to exercise a degree of influence over us. The classic example of this somewhat puzzling phenomenon is Job.

By the Lord's own admission, here was a man who was "blameless and upright, a man who fears God and shuns evil" (Job 1:8). But within the course of a few days, Job wound up losing nearly his entire family, and all of his vast possessions and holdings. Talk about going through a storm!

Yet the source of Job's personal suffering, as we know, was Satan. God allowed the Evil One to subject this righteous servant to misery for reasons we'll consider later in this chapter. The lesson to understand here, though, is that Job represented someone who had no reason to expect a storm—and yet found himself in the middle of a satanic typhoon.

The Physical Effects of Storms

After Harry Truman learned of Franklin Roosevelt's death and was sworn in as President, he made a remark characteristic of someone who's about to enter a stormy period of life. Said Truman, "I feel as though the moon, the stars, and all the planets have fallen on me."

When we experience storms in our lives, we too may feel as though we're the repository of celestial debris. We then may respond to our storm in any number of ways: in anger, fear, outrage. The physical effects of these particular emotions were outlined in previous chapters; as we saw, each was hazardous to one's health.

To this list of "storm reactions," however, we should add one more: depression, which is anger turned inward. In my clinical experience, I've found that this particular emotion is one of the most common human responses to difficult, trying circumstances. Many people come to feel that their situation is so helpless, hopeless, or threatening that they lose their resolve to weather the storm. Rejecting spiritual solutions to their problems, they slowly sink into the raging sea of depression.

In his excellent book, *How to Win Over Depression,* Dr. Tim LaHaye explains that once this sinking process begins, depression does not merely remain a state of mind. Gradually, insidiously, it can affect our physical health. He lists six principle manifestations in this regard:

1. *Erratic sleep behavior.* Sleep patterns are disturbed. Though some depressed people oversleep, it's more common for them not to be able to sleep at all.

2. *Apathy, lethargy, "the blahs."* Depression causes individuals to awake feeling tired, and to remain unmotivated throughout the day.

3. *Loss of appetite.* Food loses its appeal for the depressed. If this problem is not reversed, a person may experience serious weight loss.

4. *Loss of sex drive.* "All drive functions or basic activities come to a standstill when one is depressed," Dr. LaHaye notes. "This includes the sex drive, particularly in women. Some women have been known to get so depressed that even their menstrual function stops."

5. *Unkempt appearance.* The loss of motor drive, due to the negative self-image of the depressed person, makes individuals less concerned with matters of personal hygiene. Any number of problems—from body lice to athlete's foot—can develop as a result.

6. *Other physical ailments.* Dr. LaHaye lists several other, specific depression-related physical illnesses: tiredness, weakness, aching, dizziness, heart palpitations, tightening of

the chest, labored breathing, headache, constipation, heart-burn, and sweating (Zondervan, pp. 29-30).

Obviously, depression is an emotion with formidable physical consequences. However, it need *not* be an auto-matic, *de facto* response to life's stormy episodes. As with guilt, greed, or discontent, there are healthy—and un-healthy—ways to deal with this potentially damaging emo-tion. God *does* have a prescription for depression brought on by life's extremely difficult circumstances.

God's Prescription for Depression

We can deal with depressing situations in one of two ways. Regrettably, I find that many persons who pass through my office choose the least healthy, or "wrong" way.

This afternoon, two middle-aged sisters sat in my office as I informed them that their mother was dying from inoperable cancer. As might be imagined, they immediately burst into tears. However, they were not crying because they feared their mother's death. These two women confessed they felt *guilty;* they had been unkind and thoughtless toward their elderly mother in recent years. Now, realizing she soon would die, they regretted the sharp words they had spoken to her. They'd have done anything to keep her alive for a few more years, to make things right again.

In these women's reactions, I could see the seeds of depression being sown. Should they fail to come to terms with their storm, they'll spend the rest of their lives battling feelings of worthlessness and guilt. In short, they'll spend a good part of their time depressed.

So how *does* one "come to terms" with an emotional storm? What guidance can Scripture provide in this area?

When it came to weathering life's storms, the Apostle Paul clearly was in a class by himself. Just consider his resumé of agonizing experiences:

Five times I received from the Jews the forty lashes

minus one. Three times I was beaten with rods, once I was stoned, three times I was shipwrecked, I spent a night and a day in the open sea (2 Cor. 11:24-25).

Not once during this litany does Paul mention that his personal storms led him into depression. Instead, he sounds almost exuberant recounting the trials he's gone through. What was the key to his never-say-die attitude? Basically, Paul realized that his God was—and is—in control of every storm he encountered.

The same Lord who holds the universe in the palm of His hand is acutely aware of our trials as well. He will not allow us to be tested beyond our ability to endure various difficulties (1 Cor. 10:13). If we're aware of God's sovereignty over our storms, we have a point of reference and a source of strength to sustain us.

Paul seemed to be aware of this fact. In Acts, we find the Apostle on a ship which is passing through a terrible storm. The tempest is so severe, in fact, that Luke (who is recording these events) states, "We finally gave up all hope of being saved" (Acts 27:20). How much more ominous can you get?

At the height of the storm, however, Paul announces that God has graciously promised him that no one on this trip would be lost (vv. 23-24). How could the Lord make such an audacious promise? The answer, of course, lies in the fact that He was fully in control of the storm. He alone had the power to make it wax or wane.

Unfortunately, in our storms, we usually fail to appreciate this fact. Instead, we find ourselves identifying with the view Luke adopted: We're beyond the point of rescue. And so we settle more snugly into the armchair of frustration, fear, and depression—and simply wait for the worst to happen.

This approach obviously runs counter to what Paul is counselling. Rather than flailing our arms helplessly before the storm, we need to realize that God often puts us in such situations to draw us closer to Himself. When we recognize our weakness—when we acknowledge that our ego, pride, and ability can't rescue us—*then* we can learn to turn to God and recognize that He is the Master of the storm. The winds blow only at His commands.

A Presence in the Storm

You may be saying to yourself, *So God's in control of the storm. So I know my personal difficulties aren't just the by-product of a cold and impersonal fate. But how does that knowledge help me endure my storm?*

To provide any lasting comfort, the truth that God is in control of our difficult times is not enough. We also need to understand that God's *presence* and *care* are available to us in each of our storms.

A brief rereading of Acts 27 will show how God's personal care was manifested in Paul's particular storm: The Lord sent an angel to tell the Apostle that passengers and crew would survive the rain and waves (Acts 27:23-24). Likewise, when Daniel was confined in the lions' den (Dan. 6:22) and Peter was locked up in prison (Acts 12:11), angels appeared to administer God's protection, grace, and care.

Granted, it's probably been some time since an angel appeared in your home to help you ward off a bout of the blues. But that certainly doesn't mean God's presence is absent from your storms.

Dan, an acquaintance of mine, recently experienced one of the most painful storms a person can endure—divorce. "There were some days when I thought I wouldn't make it," he told me several weeks ago. "There were days when I looked back on my life and asked myself, *Is this what twenty years of marriage was for? To have it all go down the drain?*"

For months after his divorce, Dan traversed the no-man's-land of depression. Finally, when he thought his capacity for joy might never be regained, a friend invited him to a church service.

"I know it sounds melodramatic," Dan says, reflecting on the experience, "but when I attended that service—and subsequent ones—I finally realized that God could fill up that vacant spot in me. I knew He cared about me, and that knowledge made a world of difference."

In our storms, we're never alone. God is there, like a loving Father, to carry us when we fall.

Working on the Basics

In the spring and summer of 1984, it was impossible to live in the Chicago area without hearing about the Cubs' baseball season. The Cubs had a surprisingly fantastic season. They won the Eastern Division championship of the National League and played for their first pennant in nearly forty years. Unfortunately, the team eventually *lost* a heartbreaking fifth game to the San Diego Padres.

One day at lunch, I overheard two sports fans discussing the rise and fall of the Wrigley Field Wonders. "Well," said one, "I guess in spring training next year, they'll just have to get back to working on the basics."

Working on the basics. What an important concept for storm-beaten Christians to comprehend. When life is hurling its most vicious curve balls at us, it's crucial for us to remember the basics of our faith.

We can, for example, use storms as occasions to reestablish our personal commitment to God. At times when we seem most downcast, defeated, or depressed, we can use those opportunities to reacknowledge our absolute dependence on the Lord. Since Paul has provided us with so many good examples in this chapter, let's turn to him once more.

While scholarly dispute rages over the exact nature of Paul's "thorn in the flesh," it's fairly clear that the apostle could have responded to his problem in one of two ways. He could have gotten angry over his continuing affliction. Instead he chose to use this stormy dilemma to acknowledge his need for God and to recommit himself to His service. In so doing, the Lord told Paul:

> My grace is sufficient for you, for My power is
> made perfect in weakness (2 Cor. 12:9).

Paul's response to this revelation reflects the attitude every Christian should strive to maintain in the face of a storm:

> Therefore I will boast all the more gladly about my
> weaknesses so that Christ's power may rest on me.
> That is why, for Christ's sake, I delight in weakness,
> in insults, in hardships, in persecutions, in difficulties (2 Cor. 12:9-10).

Paul used a negative situation to learn more about a basic element of his faith. He used a storm to reestablish the relevance of his commitment to Christ.

Finally, we can respond healthily to storms by realizing a dual truth. Not only is God the *Master* of our storms, but He is *greater* than those storms. Nowhere is this fact more forcefully portrayed, I believe, than in Mark's account of Christ's miraculous walk across a storm-tossed Sea of Galilee (Mark 6:45-52).

As the waves whipped around them, and the disciples cringed in fear (how similar to our own reaction to personal crises), Jesus appeared on the water and offered His followers words of comfort. Please take note, though, of the inherent symbolism in our Lord's act: Christ *walked over* the very thing that was producing the disciples' anxiety. He could do so because, as the Creator, He was greater than any element in His creation. As our Lord, He is greater than any problem that may buffet us in His world.

God oversees, overhears, and overrules every storm we encounter. And by following His prescription in this area, our lives can acquire enriched dimensions. Our turning to God clearly will enhance our spiritual health—and that can help us avoid the physically debilitating demon, depression.

Chapter Eight
Destiny in Service

We are but as the instrument of Heaven,
Our work is not design, but destiny.
—OWEN MEREDITH
Clymenestra

After forty-five years of service to the same tool-and-die company, it came time for Howard to retire. A company dinner was held, the traditional gold watch presented. A fortnight later, Howard and his wife Bernice moved, as many older persons do, to Florida.

For the first time in nearly half a century, Howard found himself with time on his hands. He took up fishing, but after several months, tired of it; with nothing else to do, he began spending a good portion of his day around the house with Bernice. Yet Bernice had grown accustomed to spending her days alone as a housewife and had established a schedule all her own. Having her husband around was nice, she thought, but he *did* tend to get in the way. Howard eventually sensed her uneasiness and, feeling like a stranger in his own home, started taking daily walks to a nearby shopping mall. There, he'd simply sit for hours—thinking, watching, wondering—day after day.

A year and a half after receiving his gold watch, Howard was dead from cancer of the bowel.

His fate, sad to say, is not all that unusual. Every year, I see or hear of individuals who retire, but who die relatively soon thereafter. The irony of this is that many of these people were in good health prior to their retirement. So what killed them? A heretofore unknown syndrome that strikes only senior citizens?

No, not at all. In fact, even younger persons can become ill if they're afflicted with this disease. It's name? Well, it goes by several: purposelessness, stagnation, torpidity. It's a gnawing sense that one's life no longer has a sense of direction or meaning. It's the absence of a motivating destiny or aim.

Howard had lost that sense of meaning in his life. Without his work, and with no clear-cut plans for the future, his physical health gradually melted away through inactivity; this weakened his immune system and actually made his body more susceptible to the cancer.

Over the past seven chapters, we've looked at the types of emotions and attitudes which can adversely affect our spiritual and bodily health. We've also considered specific spiritual prescriptions to help eliminate or improve these ills.

But for the remainder of this book, I'd like to focus almost exclusively on examining concepts, thoughts, and dispositions that can *strengthen* our spiritual health, and thus, improve our physical well-being. I can think of no better place to start than with a discussion of how a knowledge and appreciation of God's will for our lives can lead us to new levels of health.

Plans I Have for You

Had Howard been a Christian, had he realized that God had a special purpose for his life, could he have been saved from what essayist Roger Rosenblatt calls "the hollow detachment of much of modern life"? I'm convinced he could have; and potentially, he might also have staved off serious illness.

Of course, my conclusion is based on one important assumption: that God does, in fact, have a will for His children. On this point, Scripture is helpful and clear. In the Book of Jeremiah, the Lord declares:

> For I know the plans I have for you . . . plans to prosper you and not to harm you, plans to give you hope and a future (Jer. 29:11).

In his epistles, the Apostle Paul also mentions this theme several times:

> Our goal is to measure up to God's plan for us (2 Cor. 10:13, TLB).

> I went there with definite orders from God (Gal. 2:2, TLB).

> For it is God who works in you to will and to act according to His good purpose (Phil. 2:13).

Underlying each of these verses is a single, striking truth: God has a will for our lives that He's eager to share with us. The knowledge that God *does* have a destiny for us—even if our understanding of that will is limited or incomplete—can positively effect all that we do in life. And this influence can lead us to a spiritual contentedness that's essential to good health.

Planned and Purposed

Let's assume that as a growing, maturing Christian, you believe you understand what God would have you do at this point in your life. Perhaps it's to be a college student, studying to be an engineer. Perhaps His will is for you to be a housewife, making your home available for a weekly Bible study. Perhaps as a retiree, it's to develop your long-neglected talents as a writer or painter.

In whatever we do, though, we are to keep before us the knowledge that our lives and work are a part of His divine destiny for us—and we should be living to fulfill that plan. This awareness carries with it certain implications. First, if we're to follow His will, our activities and work must be God-planned and God-purposed. This means that as we actively seek God's destiny for our lives, we plan and direct our days in such a way as to fully actualize His revealed plan for us. As the quote which opened this chapter indicates, our efforts are not to be of our making or design, but should be a conscious extension of our desire to please God. If we ignore this fact, or attempt to pursue a path in life which runs at cross-purposes with God's will, our efforts will end in frustration.

A friend recently told me the story of a young man who learned this lesson in a very painful way. For years, this man had known in his heart that God was calling him to be a pastor. Yet he also was a gifted athlete who was being courted by several professional football teams. An inner tension was consuming him. The teams were offering him hundreds of thousands of dollars to turn professional. But what was God offering him? A life of spiritual fulfillment, to be sure, but a future of sacrifice as well.

To make a long story short, this fellow chose to pursue a career in football. God had planned one thing for his life, yet he chose its opposite. By the end of his first season, though, his playing had been so disappointing that his team waived him; moreover, a number of injuries had placed him securely in the "damaged goods" category. As a consequence, no other team opted to pick up this young man's contract. Today, he's finally attending seminary, and is—believe it or not—much happier.

I know that story sounds like a terribly sensationalistic B-grade movie. But as the psalmist said, God had seen that young man from before his birth, and had scheduled each day of his life (Ps. 139:16). It was up to him to finally learn to plan and purpose his life according to that schedule. When he did, he was at peace with God and himself. The fact that he learned this truth in a rather dramatic fashion is almost immaterial. Sometimes, God needs to get our attention by bashing us over the head!

Timing is Essential

While it's true that God has a destiny for His children, we should not interpret this to mean that once we're following His will in a given situation, He'll never change our calling. The fact is, as we earnestly pursue God's will, we must allow our activities to be God-timed and even God-interrupted.

Consider the example of Amos. One day, he's a shepherd in the Judean town of Tekoa, obediently following God. The next, he's called to become a fiery prophet. Or what about George Beverly Shea? He once felt that he was fulfilling the Lord's plan for his life by selling insurance. Today, his singing reaches millions through his work with the Billy Graham Association.

I also think of John Sung. John was a Chinese gentleman who had been sent to the United States to study. While in this country, he became a Christian. Since he already had been promised a professorship at prestigious Beijing University, John initially was convinced God wanted him to work there. But as time passed, John realized that perhaps the Lord really desired to use him elsewhere.

By the time he was on a ship headed back to China, John knew that God now was calling him to full-time Christian service. On the morning he was due to dock in Shanghai, he arose early and walked to the ship's railing. There, quietly, he slipped his diplomas, medals, and fraternity keys overboard. His future of service to Jesus Christ was more important to him than a diploma or the prestige of a university position.

If God someday wanted him to return to academia, John figured, that would be fine. But he realized that God was now calling him to perform evangelistic work. John also realized that a Christian's endeavors sometimes are God-interrupted—and the Lord was interrupting a promising scholarly career so that he could follow another path.

Infused with Destiny

By striving to make our work and activities God-planned, God-purposed, God-timed, and even God-interrupted, our lives will be infused with a sense of God's destiny for us. We'll see that our every action provides us with an opportunity to be a part of His wondrous, awe-filled, divine plan. And as even secular psychologists have found, the sense of mental well-being which results from being at peace with one's place in life is an excellent preventative against illness.

Unfortunately, as Howard's case proved earlier, many people—including Christians—don't realize that God has charted a path for them (Ps. 139:3) or that He holds their futures in His hand. For such individuals, life—and their work in it—often lacks a firm sense of meaning.

Shakespeare's MacBeth spoke of life as a tale told by an idiot, full of sound and fury, signifying nothing. Similarly, many scholars have claimed that history is an endless cycle of events devoid of any true meaning. Commenting on this outlook, the French philosopher Jacques Ellul pointed out that such views inevitably affect an individual's view of himself in society. They can lead a person to feel a sense of distance from others and from his work; they ultimately can produce a sense of "absence instead of presence."

Such feelings, of course, would lead most people to despair. And in light of the physical effects of discontent and depression, it's easy to understand why these feelings often have a physically harmful impact on us.

Yet the person who knows that God has a plan for his life, who knows that history will culminate in Christ's return, is spared from such desperate wanderings. Indeed, God will keep in perfect peace those whose minds are steadfastly fixed on the reality of His gracious care (Isa. 26:3).

In My Life

Throughout our lives, it's possible to identify certain events—certain personal landmarks—that help us comprehend and appreciate God's will. A particularly memorable sermon, a personal talk with a dear friend, or a moment alone on a desolate mountain often can serve to fling open the shutters of our souls.

My own personal experiences have confirmed for me that my service to God was born in the crucible of His plan and destiny for my life. Because God knew me from my mother's womb, He preserved and protected me so that I could serve Him. I can unreservedly state that were it not for the Lord's care, I would not be alive today. And believe me, there is no more dramatic way to learn that God has a plan for your life than to be snatched from the steely jaws of death. After all, if there were no such thing as divine destiny, why was my life spared so many times? It surely could not be attributed to mere chance. As the British writer and politician Benjamin Disraeli accurately observed:

> A consistent man believes in destiny, a capricious
> man in chance (*Vivian Grey*, VI).

Even from the earliest days of my life, a merciful God was at work. Consider just a few of my childhood experiences.

When I was five, I was traveling with my family on a British passenger ship from Yokohama in Japan to Tianjin in north China. We were sailing during the winter and the Yellow Sea at that time of the year was beset by violent storms and treacherous ice floes. At one point, the ship's experienced captain indicated we surely would sink before reaching port. I'll always remember one sardonic remark he made as the ice closed in around us: "Passengers, put on your life jackets—for all the good it'll do you."

Despite the storm, we made it safely to shore. God had a plan for my life.

One year later, I was living on a mission compound in the

Shandong Province of China. Near our compound, nineteen wells had been drilled to supply the area with water. Unlike American wells, these had no stone walls around them; in effect, they were little more than holes in the ground—and my mother had constantly warned me to stay away from them. But, like any six-year-old, I couldn't resist joining in the fun when other missionary children began throwing rocks into the wells to hear the hollow eerie sound they made when they hit the water.

One time, though, a friend and I were playing near a large well which was very close to two smaller ones. As my pal tossed a rock into the large well, I jumped back to avoid being hit and fell right into one of the other wells.

I realized immediately how serious my predicament was. The bottle-shaped well was filled with about five to six feet of water, and I was barely able to keep my nose above the surface. Desperately, I sought a toehold in the center of the well where we had been throwing rocks.

Meanwhile, the boy who had caused my unexpected trip ran off to tell my mother what had happened. However, he was so shook up by the incident he couldn't remember *which* well I had dropped into. So my mother dashed outside and started checking *each* of the nineteen holes. To add to the confusion—as if things weren't bad enough—the wells were fed by an underground spring which caused little air bubbles to rise to the surface. As my poor mother peered down each well, she couldn't tell whether the bubbles were coming from the spring, or from her son's lungs. Wisely, she simply kept yelling out my name until I finally managed to croak out a "Help."

Needless to say, I was rescued. God had a plan for my life.

Not long thereafter, I found myself flat on my back suffering from diphtheria during an epidemic that had infected many students at the boarding school I attended. Though relatively rare in the U.S., diphtheria, in its worst stage, causes a membrane to form over the airway in the back of the victim's throat. Death by suffocation usually results. If the victim is lucky enough to survive suffocation, diphtheria still can strike in another deadly manner: by inflaming the muscle of the heart. Death then occurs through myocarditis, a weakening of the heart muscle.

Fortunately, I responded to the treatment I received. God had a plan for my life.

In 1940, after being evacuated from China, my family and I were headed by train to Philadelphia. My father had relatives in that city and had planned a short visit for us there. In the same car with us, however, was a convicted murderer who was being transported to a penitentiary back East.

As I sat passively in my seat, watching the scenery roll by, I suddenly heard a commotion several seats behind us. A second later, gunfire erupted. Before I could react, a bullet whizzed inches over my head and crashed against the window ahead of me. It seems the convict had decided to execute an escape—a successful one, I might add—and in the course of his unscheduled exit, had discharged a weapon that he had wrestled from his guard.

Luckily for me, I did not become another of his murder victims. God had a plan for my life.

Well, after all the excitement of those first few years, I actually managed to reach my thirteenth birthday before I found myself in another interesting situation. Following the Second World War, my family and I returned to China—but not without some adventure along the way.

We had left Pensacola, Florida, sailed through the Panama Canal, and docked temporarily in San Diego. That's where our problems began. You see, the ship's crew was given shore leave and, as sailors are sometimes wont to do, they got extremely drunk. At the same time, a group of labor union organizers were in San Diego, and they had a fine time inciting our drunken crew to revolt against their management—namely, our ship's captain.

Well, a mob of rowdy sailors soon descended on the ship, which was, at the time, being refueled. Naturally, this fueling operation provided them with a perfect opportunity to throw lit matches into the fuel holds in an attempt to blow up the ship. As if this activity weren't felonious enough for them, one sailor proceeded to stab the ship's engineer. While mutiny raged below us, we barricaded ourselves in our cabin.

Finally, the captain produced a pistol, and, after firing a few well-aimed warning shots, succeeded in getting the crew quieted down to the point where we could set sail. Needless to say, a somewhat tense atmosphere prevailed on board during the remainder of our voyage; it worsened perceptibly when word leaked out that the captain had arranged a little court-martial for his crew upon their arrival in the Orient. Graciously, our captain advised us to stay indoors as much as possible, emphasizing that some crazed sailor might just decide to vent his frustrations by skewering a luckless passenger or two.

For the rest of the trip we were extremely cautious about where we went, and managed to arrive at our destination all in one piece. But then, I shouldn't have been too surprised by that. After all, God had a plan for my life.

More recently my son and I were kayaking around St. John's Island in the Caribbean when we were suddenly faced with very heavy winds and waves fifteen feet in height. Physically exhausted, we had paddled steadily into the wind for five hours to keep off the rocky coastline. Finally a large wave turned us over. All my manuevering and thrashing failed to free me from my entrapped position in the upturned kayak. God helped my son rescue me just at the last moment. I saw again God's plan in my life was not completed.

The Lesson

Hopefully, it won't take falling into a well or surviving a mutiny to convince you that God has a purpose and plan for you. And hopefully, you won't succumb to the belief that our God is too small to overcome the perplexity and purposelessness that oppress so many people. As J.B. Phillips once observed:

> The trouble with many people today is that they
> have not found a God big enough for modern
> needs. While their experience of life has grown in
> a score of directions, and their mental horizons
> have been expanded to the point of bewilderment
> by world events and scientific discoveries, their
> ideas of God have remained largely static (*Your
> God Is Too Small,* Wyvern Books, p. 7).

Remember that there's a purpose and reason for all of your
activities. That purpose is to bring glory and praise to God, to
enjoy His fellowship, and to serve Him with God-centered
and God-directed obedience. In short, we are to seek His will
and our destiny.

The inner peace and contentedness that this type of lifestyle produce are crucial to the maintenance of good health.
Patients I've seen—who've acknowledged the truths outlined
in this chapter—often are able to ward off the types of
attitudes and dispositions which we've seen can lead to
illness.

Knowing you have a destiny in Christ Jesus can add years
to your health and health to your years. Are you experiencing God's plan for your life?

Chapter Nine
Think About Such Things

At best, I could be described as an extremely infrequent television viewer. Yet on those rare occasions when I do watch TV, I find that shows which center around hospitals or doctors hold an odd fascination for me. It's certainly not the high-tech settings or the "dedicated young professionals" that intrigue me. (I get enough exposure to operating rooms and surgeons as it is.) No, what I find most interesting is the types of illnesses featured on these programs.

I once heard a media consultant say that television doesn't necessarily seek to *reflect* reality—it strives to *create* its own. And if the types of ailments paraded across our TV screens are intended to represent illnesses common in this country, that consultant's observation was right on target. What I mean is, television medical programs love to concentrate on patients with exotic, life-threatening, unknown diseases—which is only understandable. After all, it probably would be difficult to wring a great deal of pathos out of a plot which dealt with one woman's lifelong battle to overcome hay fever.

The fact is, TV goes for *excitement*. That's why we get sagas about mysterious microbes that run amok at secret government research labs, and stories about diseases that only affect tourists who wade in the Ganges River.

But that is *not* real life. The vast majority of my patients don't come to me suffering from the sort of horrible infirmities cooked up by West Coast scriptwriters. Actually, I'd estimate that a full 85 percent of the people for whom I provide medical services come to me with much more run-of-the-mill ailments: ulcers, high blood pressure, bad hearts. And a primary reason I see these illnesses is *not* because my patients have been splashing about in the Ganges, but because many of them are afflicted with one or more of the emotions we've discussed in this book: anger, worry, guilt, depression.

Throughout this book, I've tried to devote a fair amount of space to describing the various physical complications produced by such attitudes and emotions. Yet as you read the chapter on greed, for example, it probably occurred to you that not everyone who is covetous winds up with alopecia. That fact leads us to a very reasonable question. What factor determines whether a spiritually based illness will result in a serious physical ailment or merely a mild one?

I believe that profound ill health is much more likely to occur when a person *fixates* such negative emotions as discontent, fear, or greed. This interpretation would partially explain why Rockefeller suffered from alopecia; his preoccupation with money bordered on being a twenty-four-hour-a-day pursuit. He dwelt upon his greedy impulses until they seriously damaged his health.

Thus, an important reason why anger, worry, or hate can lead to serious sickness is because the individual afflicted with that attitude often dwells on it continually. *Fixating on negative emotions* can fuel an illness and even determine the degree of its severity.

Don't Look to the World

Realizing that our thoughts can affect our health is an important first step toward achieving spiritual and physical well-being. But if you're interested in finding a prescription that will get your thought life back on track, don't look to the world for it. Unfortunately, we're surrounded by influences which only serve to aggravate personal problems.

Just pause for a moment to consider the various things in life that can keep us in a negative frame of mind.

Yesterday, Tony—who suffers from a hot temper (and, not surprisingly, from a duodenal ulcer)—received his monthly checking account statement. When he saw that a $30 service charge had been slapped on two returned checks, he was ready to hit the roof. Because his wife had written the bad checks (albeit accidentally), he yelled at her, threatened to take her name off the account, and generally behaved like an ogre. For people who already have trouble controlling their anger, receiving bad financial information usually reinforces that emotion and makes it easier to fixate on.

Martha has just had a fight with her best friend and is feeling depressed about it. In an effort to get her mind off her problems, she switches on the nightly news. Then, she hears of another terrorist bombing in the Middle East, a fatal chemical leak in a Third World country, and a bus accident in the Midwest that killed a dozen school children.

What cheery information! What a marvelous way to break out of feeling blue! Let's face it: The news media really can make a depressed person feel even worse about life. As Roger Campbell has noted in his book, *Staying Positive in a Negative World:*

> Today, we have the dubious privilege of knowing about nearly everything that is wrong with the world every day. We are plugged into the news gathering services of the entire planet, and if not careful, we will find ourselves carrying burdens enough to break us down (Victor Books, p. 30).

In essence, we are surrounded by a society that doesn't exactly generate situations conducive to good emotional health. Reviewing one author's recent novel, *Newsweek* magazine noted that the writer depicted the world as a place in which "occult supermarket tabloids are joined with TV disaster footage as household staples providing nourishment and febrile distraction."

The most sobering fact about such observations, of course, is that by being bombarded by such adverse stimuli, our emotional and spiritual problems can snowball to monstrous proportions. And the end result of that process, as we've seen time and time again, often is ill health.

Other Attitudes

My reason for reviewing a few of the factors that can exacerbate negative thoughts was not to provide you with *more* means by which to injure your health. On the contrary, it simply was to point out that influences exist in the world of which we're often unaware—influences that keep us dwelling on hurtful thoughts or emotions. Roger Campbell, for example, admits that it took him years to realize that his addiction to listening to news programs was a prime factor behind his feelings of constant stress.

Thus, examining such influences actually can have a positive outcome. So can briefly reviewing several other emotions not previously touched on in this book; if constantly dwelt upon or thought about, these feelings can lead to their own set of illnesses.

Loss

Janet was a Panamanian woman who worked at Gorgas Hospital in the Canal Zone while I was completing my internship and surgical residency. She had fallen in love with one of the American interns at the hospital and, apparently, there had been some talk of marriage between them. However, when the young man's internship was over, not only did he *not* marry Janet, he returned to the United States without her. It's not difficult to imagine how Janet felt. Apart from her feelings of betrayal, she also experienced a tremendous sense of loss. Here was a man whom she'd loved, with whom she'd wanted to spend her life. Now he was gone.

Eventually, she developed severe ulcerative colitis—which required emergency surgery and the removal of her entire colon. For six weeks after the operation she hovered between life and death. Fortunately, she survived. But it was clear to the people who knew Janet that her grave state had been brought about by her dwelling on a deep personal loss.

Sandy also knew what it meant to experience loss. Shortly before her sophomore year of college, her father died from a massive, unexpected heart attack. She and her dad had never really been close, but in the years before his death, they'd really begun to understand one another better; the seeds of a loving and lasting relationship had been planted. Now Sandy grieved for the years she had wasted with her father and for the years they'd never have. For months after the funeral, Sandy's appetite decreased almost to the vanishing point; her nights were filed with fitful sleep. Sandy had suffered a tragic loss, and as her thoughts constantly returned to that loss, its effects were recorded on her physical health.

Stress

Stress has gotten some bad press in recent years. Actually, stress isn't always a bad thing to experience. Studies have shown, for example, that some employees' work output and efficiency *improves* when they're subjected to situations of mild pressure. Similarly, to prepare its crews to handle emergency situations, the U.S. Navy now is requiring seamen to pass a rigorous test. Water is forcefully pumped into a mock submarine or ship's hull, and sailors must successfully seal hatchways and take other appropriate measures as thousands of gallons of water splash around them. The aim of the exercise is to create the type of stressful environment that would reign on a ship that actually was sinking. Reports indicate the program has been a great success.

Yet by and large, in our society, stress usually doesn't perform such salutary functions. Instead, by living day in and day out with pressure, by allowing our minds to be occupied with stressful thoughts ("I'll never get this term paper written in time," "How will I ever manage to pay my mortgage this month?" "I just *know* my boss will hate the work I'm doing"), our bodies pay a heavy toll.

A *Peanuts* cartoon I saw recently was very revealing. Charlie Brown is watching television as his little sister, Sally, announces, "I think I have too much stress in my life. I think my arteries are closing. If you'd do my homework for me, it would reduce my stress." Charlie Brown tells her to get back to work, and in the last panel we see Sally, slumped over her desk, groaning, "You can't do good homework when you can feel your arteries closing."

In a humorous way, this cartoon concisely summarizes the hazards of excess stress. The more we fixate on the stressful aspects of life, the more likely we are to open ourselves up to such anxiety-related problems as impotence, regional ileitis—a swelling and infection of the small intestine—and essential hypertension.

Life Changes

Several years ago, researchers created what has come to be known as the Stress Index Chart. On this chart, "life change unit points" are assigned to typical life events, and the more points a person scores, the more likely he or she is to experience a major health change. For example, an individual who recently has been married can award himself fifty points for that experience. A change in work hours or conditions scores twenty points, and a change in one's financial state earns thirty-eight points. (For the complete list see: Jan Markell with Jane Winn, *Overcoming Stress,* Victor Books, pp. 90-91.) A person scoring 300 points or more on this index probably is heading for serious physical trouble.

While we may not always be able to prevent changes from coming into our lives—such as the death of a close family member (worth sixty-three points)—we can avoid their potentially devastating effects by not constantly worrying or thinking about them.

Alan is someone who needs to take this bit of advice to heart. He's frankly admitted to me that he spends an abnormal amount of time thinking about the future and what it holds. He wonders, for instance, whether another severe economic recession would force him out of his present job, whether that would necessitate his moving to another part of the country, and how such changes would affect his marriage. By dwelling on just these *three* potential life changes, Alan easily could score over 200 points on a Stress Index Chart.

It's all too easy for us to worry about tomorrow and its unknown qualities. But we must remember that fixating on such concerns can damage our health. Let us not forget James' admonishment:

> Now listen, you who say, "Today or tomorrow we will go to this or that city, spend a year there, carry on business and make money." Why, you do not even know what will happen tomorrow. What is your life? You are a mist that appears for a little while and then vanishes (James 4:13-14).

Developing Healthy Thoughts

God wants us to experience life to its fullest (John 10:10) and to enjoy a peace "which transcends all understanding" (Phil 4:7). How can we do this? The Apostle Paul outlines God's prescription in one incredible verse:

> Finally, brothers, whatever is true, whatever is noble, whatever is right, whatever is pure, whatever is lovely, whatever is admirable—if anything

is excellent or praiseworthy—think about such
things (Phil. 4:8).

I've found that Christians respond to this verse in various
ways. In thinking about what is noble and true, some like to
reflect on Christ's work of redemption, on how God became
man so that our sins would be forgiven and our fellowship
with the Eternal One reestablished. Others meditate on the
majesty of His creation, as did the psalmist:

When I consider Your heavens, the work of Your
fingers, the moon and the stars, which You have
set in place, what is man that You are mindful of
him? (Ps. 8:3-4)

I've found it particularly rewarding to dwell on God's
attributes. While in Ethiopia, I had to run a 105-bed hospital
nearly single-handedly for four of my eight years there. At
such times, it would have been easy for me to get discour-
aged, to worry about supplies and personnel, to have become depressed over not being able to cure every patient. It
would have been easy to dwell on the negative elements of
my work there.

But it was in such situations that I discovered God's prescription for oppressive thoughts. When I thought about the
Lord's characteristics—His marvelous attributes—the negative thoughts that had so rudely intruded into my life were
washed away. Damaging emotions and attitudes were wondrously expelled once they were exposed to the healing
presence of God.

This is no mysterious process. Actually, it's rather logical.
The grandeur of God simply is more appealing to dwell on
than the vagaries and malice of life. The wise person realizes
this and seeks to direct his thoughts accordingly (Ps. 1:2).

An exposition of the Lord's attributes obviously could
constitute a book in itself, and many fine volumes dealing
with this subject already have been written. For now,

though, please simply consider the following list a starting point for your own devotional study.

Our Lord is:

- Holy (Lev. 20:26)
- Righteous ((Ps. 85:13)
- Just (Deut. 32:4)
- Faithful (Gen. 28:15)
- Eternal (Deut. 33:27)
- Always Present (Jer. 23:23-24)
- All-Powerful (Jer. 32:17)
- All-Knowing (Ps. 147:5)
- Unchanging (Heb. 13:8)
- Loving (Ps. 63:3)

Traveling across Africa, I saw sunsets that were unparalleled in beauty. Attempting to describe them in words would be an exercise in futility. So it is with trying precisely to define God's attributes. The ten words I've used here can only approximate a description of who and what He is. And even then, God's traits take on different meanings in the context of our individual lives. For me, His faithfulness could bring to mind thoughts of His provision during years of missionary service. For you, it might suggest His abiding presence during a particularly difficult trial.

But in a way, our inability to weave an eloquent and exhaustive description of God is a blessing. As we focus on His attributes, our minds are challenged to explore each nuance of their meaning. We're motivated to learn how we can apply the truth of His holiness to our own quest for righteous living. We're inspired to search out the implications of His omnipresence and omniscience. We're spurred on to comtemplate the depths of His love.

In a world of transient emotions—where problems besiege us one day, only to disappear the next—our Lord's attributes never change. He is always the same (Heb. 13:8). "I am the Lord, I change not" (Mal. 3:6, KJV).

The Results

By thinking about things which are true, noble, right, pure, lovely, admirable, excellent, and praiseworthy, and by dwelling on the attributes of God, we're able to end our fixation on the hurtful and harmful emotions of life. By directing our minds to that which occupies a heavenly plane, we can overcome the debilitating physical illnesses which hatred, greed, and worry engender.

I recall the experience of a man who'd been a patient of mine for several years. He was in for a routine checkup, and I noticed his blood pressure was dangerously elevated. I mentioned this to him, and he immediately had an explanation for it.

He had taken his invalid father into his home ten years ago and had cared for him ever since. Yet when his father died a month ago, my patient learned that all insurance benefits had been willed to *another* son—a son who hadn't even *visited* his father during his long illness.

My patient was, to say the least, extremely angry over his brother's having received the entire inheritance. After hearing this story, I told him I could give him medication to lower his blood pressure. However, I also mentioned that he'd have to live with its numerous side effects, as the dosage would need to be fairly strong to overcome his feelings of hatred and bitterness.

Then I told him, "You know, there is another way. There's God's way. He's told us that He can give us the strength to forgive a brother seventy times seven.

"If you really want to get better," I continued, "stop dwelling on how cheated you feel. I can understand that you're angry. But by thinking about God's goodness, you can triumph over those feelings. Think about Him, and you won't need to take these pills for the rest of your life."

He decided to follow the prescription Paul outlined in Philippians; at the end of one year, I took him off his medication. He hasn't required it since.

His experience shows that thought patterns can't always

be transformed overnight. Exchanging harmful thoughts for holy ones usually takes time. But the fact remains that after this man committed himself to the process of dwelling on the thoughts outlined in Philippians 4:8, his physical health improved.

By focusing our thoughts and desires on God's attributes and His will, we are well on the way to overcoming the diseases brought on by negative emotions.

Why not begin a new life right now? Why not choose to think about our Lord's wonderful attributes today?

Chapter Ten
The Master's Touch

The term *world view* has become fairly fashionable in recent years. Mission boards, for example, are asking prospective missionaries to explain how their world view affects their understanding of evangelism. At congresses of socially concerned Christians, believers are encouraged to develop a world view which is sensitive to the needs of the poor.

But what exactly does this trendy phrase mean? And what does it have to do with the relationship between our spiritual and physical health?

Broadly defined, a world view represents the way a person perceives the universe and his place in it. It is the sum of the answers a person gives to certain basic questions; in a recent magazine article, writer and editor Jim Sire suggested several such questions: What is ultimate reality? What is the status of the universe? What is a human being? What is the meaning of our human sojourn on earth?

These queries are not merely the province of bearded, pipe-smoking philosophers. How we answer them determines such matters as whether we believe in God, whether we acknowledge that a divine destiny exists for our lives, and whether we trust God with our daily affairs. Our personal world view determines how we look at life; it is on this crucial point that we'll eventually build an analysis of how our world view affects our physical and spiritual health.

Two World Views

"We saw giants out there! And we saw a single cluster of grapes that was so big it took *two* men to carry it. But forget about the grapes! I'm telling you, we saw *giants!*"

What? Are these the rantings of some drug-crazed lunatic? More than once I've seen persons brought into the emergency room, who, under the influence of some illegal narcotic, witnessed hallucinations. But that was not the case here. No, these words came from the mouths of men who were entirely sober.

As Israel was preparing to enter the Promised Land, the Lord commanded Moses to send out twelve scouts "to explore the land of Canaan" (Num. 13:2). Once this was done, the scouts were to report back on the status of Canaan's geography, demography, and agricultural prospects.

While in Canaan, the twelve saw the enormous grapes and concluded that this part of the Middle East was a land that flowed "with milk and honey" (v. 27). Only one slight snag prevented Israel from immediately occupying this choice piece of real estate: A people known as the Nephilim lived there. And, according to the intrepid scouts' consensus, these people were giants: "We seemed like grasshoppers in our own eyes, and we looked the same to them" (Num. 13:33). On the basis of the Nephilim's imposing presence, ten of the twelve scouts quickly decided that Israel should steer clear of Canaan.

Joshua and Caleb were the two scouts who dissented from this recommendation. In fact, Caleb rather succinctly made his case for moving into the Promised Land by proclaiming: "We should go up and take possession of the land, for we can certainly do it" (Num. 13:30).

Very interesting. All twelve scouts saw the same fortified cities in Canaan. All twelve men looked upon the same burly

Nephilim. So why had Joshua and Caleb concluded there was nothing to worry about? Why were they insisting that Israel should proceed into the Promised Land as planned? Quite simply, these two scouts held a world view that differed significantly from their colleagues.

When Joshua and Caleb looked into Canaan, they didn't just see giants. They didn't just focus on the apparent impossibilities of the situation. They saw a land that God had promised to them and they viewed the future, accordingly, through eyes of faith. Their compatriots' world view, by contrast, apparently was influenced by a belief that the mighty God who had parted the Red Sea would be no match for a bunch of oversized Canaanites.

Why the Difference?

It behooves us to examine the foundations of Caleb and Joshua's world view. After all, every day, we're confronted with our own "giants"—many of which involve our struggles with physical illness. We need, therefore, to understand what these two heroes of the faith understood.

Basically, Joshua and Caleb must have asked themselves the same type of questions Jim Sire outlined earlier. They must have thought about ultimate reality and considered the purpose of their existence. Based on the things they'd witnessed during their lifetimes—divinely-sent plagues, the Exodus, the provision for Israel in the wilderness—they must have been able to conclude that God was utterly worthy of their trust and devotion. This knowledge, then, was the foundation of their world view.

Joshua and Caleb gave testimony to their particular view of life in a speech made before the assembled throngs of Israel. Though the people already had decided to side with the ten scouts, Joshua and Caleb said:

> If the Lord is pleased with us, He will lead us into
> the land. . . . And do not be afraid of the people of

the land, because we will swallow them up. Their protection is gone, but the Lord is with us (Num. 14:8-9).

In essence, these two courageous men were claiming that they could be confident about the future because they served a God who loves His children, protects them, always is with them, and performs miracles on their behalf (Num. 14:11). Their world view enabled them to live lives of certainty and faith.

World Views and Health

You still may be puzzled as to what one's world view has to do with good health. As we've seen throughout this book, good spiritual health is one key to sound physical health. As you accept that premise, you'll begin to realize that your personal world view is immensely important. For to enjoy spiritual and thus, physical health, our minds must be attuned to a world view that mirrors the one held by Joshua and Caleb. Like them, we too must see God as loving, abiding, protective, and miraculous.

But to develop our world view along these lines, we must spend time meditating on who God is. For when greed, anger, or fear confront us—and threaten us with their illnesses—we need to possess a view of life that embraces the crucial characteristics of our God; one of the Lord's magnificent attributes must be deeply engrained in our world concept.

And what is this attribute? God's healing power.

The issue of divine healing has tended to divide the body of Christ into two opposing camps. One side believes miraculous healing ended along with the Apostolic Age; the other contends that this gift is operative today.

Those who know me probably would characterize me as a theological conservative, and that's a label with which I'm fairly comfortable. Unfortunately, the tag *conservative* often is associated with a disbelief in miraculous, divine activity in the present age.

I believe, however, that God still heals people—both physically and spiritually. I've no reason to doubt that our Lord's well-documented healing ministry has been suspended in the 1980s. This does not mean, of course, that I endorse every professed "faith healer" who comes down the pike. Nor do I believe that supernatural healing necessarily requires the intervention of a human intermediary, though in certain instances, this may be appropriate.

But I am convinced that at times, our physical, mental, and spiritual health only can be salvaged by the touch of Jesus Christ Himself. When we are faced by disease, sometimes the only way we can pass successfully through it is to rely on the God who understands our frailty and who gives us life.

Our timeless and divine God *can* intervene in our daily lives. He *can* reach down and touch our bodies when we are wracked with illness. An acknowledgment of this fact is a virtual prerequisite to receiving any of the Lord's prescriptions for health.

Two Reactions to Disease

Anyone who's seen *Ben-Hur* wlll remember one poignant scene that occurred toward the end of the film. Ben-Hur's mother and sister are afflicted with leprosy, and as he attempts to find help for them, the family wanders through a sparsely peopled town square. However, as soon as the locals see Ben-Hur's mother and sister, they begin to shout, "Lepers! Unclean! Lepers!" and start hurling stones at them.

In Maryland several months ago, a five-year-old boy was diagnosed as having herpes sores on his face and hands. Once parents and students at the school he attended learned of his condition, they reacted angrily They demanded that the "herpes kid" be kept out of school, lest he infect his classmates.

Most of us react very poorly to disease. We are repulsed by

the ravages of cancer; we are sickened by the deformities that characterize some classes of illness. Jesus' behavior, however, stands in stark contrast to our own.

Our Lord willingly touched lepers (Luke 5:12-13) and sore-infested paralytics (Mark 2:1-5). No matter how vile the disease, Jesus looked beyond the pock scars, past the gnarled limbs, to the *person* who was ill. Indeed, Mark notes that "He healed many, so that those with diseases were pushing forward to touch Him" (Mark 3:10). In essence, Jesus took the world's notion of how to react to the infirm and wretched, and stood it on its ear. He boldly demonstrated that He would reach out to heal anyone who believed in Him, no matter how dire their circumstances.

That fact bears repeating. Jesus would heal anyone who believed, no matter how terrible or hopeless their disease appeared. Now apply the truth of that statement to *spiritual* illnesses. Perhaps even now, you feel as though you have a spiritual illness that's too hideous to show anyone. Perhaps your greed has led you to cheat innocent coworkers or to lie on your income tax return. Perhaps your anger has wounded people who truly care for you. Perhaps you feel that your discontent, your depression, or your guilt is too deeply embedded in your soul ever to be healed.

Before you go any further, just consider this:

> A man with leprosy came to [Jesus] and begged Him on his knees, "If You are willing, You can make me clean."
>
> Filled with compassion, Jesus reached out His hand and touched the man. "I am willing," He said. "Be clean!"
>
> Immediately, the leprosy left him and he was cured (Mark 1:40-42).

This passage shows that God is willing and able to reach out to us at all times. We don't need to rely on our own inner strength to overcome hurtful emotions and their physical consequences. God already has the necessary strength for us. Even if others have recoiled from us after seeing our spiritual illness, God *can* reach out and touch us.

Identification and Compassion

God also heals us because He understands how miserable illness is, and this knowledge evokes His compassion. Again, this principle operates on both a physical and spiritual level.

Scripture doesn't indicate whether Jesus was ever actually sick. But it's a truism that you don't have to personally experience an illness to know how painful it is. A person doesn't need to suffer from leukemia in order to sympathize with the sufferer. Such obviously was the case when Jesus came upon an invalid at the pool called Bethesda.

As John notes, the scene at the pool was one that would have touched anyone's heart:

> Here a great number of disabled people used to lie—the blind, the lame, the paralyzed. One who was there had been an invalid for thirty-eight years (John 5:3-5).

Jesus must have been powerfully moved by this one invalid's condition. Can you imagine it? For close to four decades, this man had been unable to walk. Day after day, he lay by the pool at the Sheep Gate hoping, perhaps, for a few charitable coins to be tossed his way—dreaming, perhaps, that the God of his fathers would show him mercy.

Jesus immediately responded to the misery of this situation by healing the man. And what is the lesson to be learned here? Simply, our Lord's humanity enabled Him to share in the depths of this individual's suffering; His divinity allowed Him to put an end to it.

Christ held a special place in His heart for the world's sick and dispossessed, as each of the Gospel writers clearly attest. Could it be that as the One who would be "despised and rejected of men," He felt an acute empathy for persons who themselves were shunned on account of their illnesses?

Let us never forget that Jesus fully understands our sicknesses. As the writer of Hebrews points out, "He too shared in their humanity. . . . He Himself suffered" (Heb. 2:14, 18). Thus, when our illnesses are the outgrowth of such emotions as anger, or greed, we must remember that these are emotions which our Lord observed firsthand. He witnessed Peter's anger in the Garden of Gethsemane; He knew that Judas' greed could be satiated by thirty pieces of silver. He *can,* therefore, heal us from illnesses of the soul and set us free from their effects on our bodies.

Recipients of His Love

Finally, I believe God heals us simply to express His love. A coworker of mine told me that on the way home from the hospital the other day, he impulsively decided to stop by a florist to buy some flowers for his wife. When he got home and presented the surprise bouquet to her, she became mildly suspicious.

"Alright," she said, "it's not my birthday or our anniversary. What're the flowers for? Are you planning to go to a convention or something without me? Is this to butter me up?"

"Not at all," my colleague replied, slipping his arms around her waist. "I just wanted to tell you I love you."

In a somewhat similar fashion, God has given us His prescriptions for health and His healing touch as indications of how much He loves us. The Apostle John tells us that God "so loved the world" that He sent His only Son to be our salvation (John 3:16). And yet, important as Jesus' arrival on earth was, God did not limit His expression of love to that single pivotal act. Rather, He also demonstrated His love by placing the breathtaking wonders of creation around us, by instituting the sacred union of marriage, and by leaving His Holy Spirit with us. And, importantly, He continues to show us His love and compassion through the priceless gift of divine healing.

The Master's touch is not a commodity to be purchased (Acts 8:18-19), but an extension of a divine attribute concisely recorded in 1 John: "God is love" (4:8). The only "payment" God requires in return for His healing grace is our thankfulness. Luke makes note of this point in recounting the story of the ten lepers:

> Now on His way to Jerusalem . . . ten men who had leprosy met Him. They stood at a distance and called out in a loud voice, "Jesus, Master, have pity on us!"
>
> When He saw them, He said, "Go, show yourselves to the priests." And as they went, they were cleansed.
>
> One of them, when he saw he was healed, came back, praising God in a loud voice. He threw himself at Jesus' feet and thanked Him—and he was a Samaritan.
>
> Jesus asked, "Were not all ten cleansed? Where are the other nine? Was no one found to return and give praise to God except this foreigner?" (Luke 17:11-18)

This narrative contains several important lessons. First, it reinforces the point that God simply asks us to thank Him for His healing touch. But it also testifies to the three main reasons outlined earlier in this chapter as to why God heals.

In this story, the relationship between Christ's desire to heal and the world's reaction to illness is evident. Note that the lepers "stood at a distance" as they made their request for healing. Lepers just couldn't walk up to someone and expect a warm welcome; their unsightly sores would have made them the target of verbal and physical abuse. If for no other reason than this, Jesus was predisposed to heal them.

But by seeing their wretched condition, a second impulse

was touched off in our Lord: He felt compassion for them. He wanted these lepers to enjoy a full life, as He wants for all His children (John 10:10). Yet He recognized that as long as their deformities persisted, those ten men would remain outcasts. He responded to their request and cleansed them.

Finally, Jesus' healing activity showed that He loved the lepers—and this love was expressed in a twofold way. First, Christ's divine healing of the lepers was an act of unselfish, compassionate caring. By simply relieving these individuals of leprosy's discomforts, He showed them the depths of His love. Yet by instructing them to present themselves to the priests—who certainly would quiz them about their amazing recovery—Jesus was introducing the lepers to the reality of who He was. He was the Messiah who had come to "proclaim freedom for the prisoners and recovery of sight for the blind" (Luke 4:18). Who else could have healed them? When a person acknowledges and accepts these truths, he or she becomes a recipient of God's everlasting love.

The Master's Touch

Hopefully, as you review this chapter, you'll find yourself with a world view that fully appreciates God's capacity and motivations for healing. And once the reality of His ability to touch our bodies is incorporated into our lives, we'll be able to grasp the *spiritual* benefits of His touch.

Christ's touch can bring us inner peace as our sins are taken away and buried in the deepest sea. We can experience a sense of renewed dignity as His children. And His touch should motivate us to recognize His absolute ownership over our lives. We need to respond to these realizations with wholehearted obedience and service to Him.

In light of all these considerations, doesn't it make sense to seek the Master's healing touch on a daily basis?

(**Editor's Note:** For a more thorough study of the subject of divine healing, refer to Richard Sipley's *Understanding Divine Healing,* published by Victor Books.)

Chapter Eleven
Prescriptions for Better Health

Any number of factors can prevent a prescription from being taken promptly and properly. At least once a week, for instance, an apologetic patient will call to ask me to reorder a prescription that accidentally was spilled down the drain, dropped into a fish tank, or crushed by a trash compactor.

Other prescriptions have met even more bizarre fates. During my tenure at the mission hospital in Soddo, Ethiopia, I found that wild animals occasionally managed to eat boxes of our medicine before they could be properly stored. I can't help but think that a lot of very healthy hyenas must be running around Africa right now.

And sadly, I also recall how some Ethiopians would ask for prescription refills, only to trade the valuable medication for money, clothing, or food on the black market.

However, the most common way in which a prescription is misapplied, is when the directions for its usage are misread or misinterpreted. Needless to say, I wouldn't want that to happen to someone who's taking God's prescriptions for health. Perhaps it would be prudent, then, to make sure the directions for this particular brand of "medication" are clear.

I'm certain you've all seen medicinal labels that read, "Not to be taken with any other forms of medication." This warning is posted to prevent patients from mixing medications that could have counteracting or dangerous side effects. The wonderful thing about God's prescriptions, though, is that this rule doesn't apply. Such palliatives as confession, forgiveness, and faith all can be ingested at the same time without any negative effects. In fact, the *more* of them you take, the better off your soul and body will be!

Hopefully, you've already started using God's prescriptions for health, and are beginning to notice the difference they can make in your life. However, I realize we *have* covered quite a bit of material in this book, and I wouldn't want these prescriptions to lead to a case of mental indigestion.

So in the days, weeks, and months ahead, as you carefully consider each aspect of God's prescriptions, I'd like to leave you with four simple questions to ponder. By thinking about these biblically based questions, you'll be able to focus more clearly on the major themes and prescriptions presented in this book. And as you meditate on the answers you give to these queries, you'll be fortified with a healthy spirit—a spirit that can lead to better physical health.

"Is Anything Too Hard for the Lord?" (Gen. 18:14)

Why do so many people seem to think that certain situations are just too difficult for God to handle? As we noted earlier, the Israelites expressed this very attitude when their backs were to the Red Sea and Pharaoh was hot on their trail. They were certain that God could do nothing to reverse their desperate plight.

One of the problems with such a view, of course, is that it implies that God's ability to heal our bodies also is stunted. As I've heard some of my patients say, "Take God's prescription for health? I don't know. God's pretty busy; He's got His hands full as it is. I'm sure there's nothing He can do about my colon."

Nothing could be further from the truth. God is intimately interested in every aspect of our souls and bodies; He's even numbered the hairs on our heads! (Matt. 10:30) Nothing is too difficult for God to accomplish. He's repeatedly demonstrated the truth of this fact in my life.

In 1975, my family and I received permission from the Marxist Ethiopian government to leave that country. Early one spring morning, we left Soddo in our Fiat station wagon and set off across the desert to Addis Ababa, the capital city. Nearly an hour into the trip, however, our car broke down. As if being stuck in the desert weren't bad enough, we also were stranded in a section of the country populated by the Arrussi tribe—a naturally fierce people whom the government had made even meaner through steady doses of anti-Western propaganda. As a matter of fact, a week earlier, I had treated the occupants of a marooned Landrover who'd been attacked by Arrussi tribesmen about nine miles from our present location.

Miles from civilization and with unpredictable Arrussis roaming the region, I began to consider the very real possibility that this might be the end of the line for us. I wondered, *Will the God who never sleeps, the Lord who keeps the planets spinning in their orbits, have time to help a carload of stranded missionaries?*

Even as these thoughts whirred through my mind, I heard a rumbling noise in the distance. *Oh, no,* I thought. *It's the Arrussis. They've spotted us.* The rumbling grew increasingly louder and my heart pounded as I waited for an Arrussi welcoming committee to arrive. A second later, the source of the rumbling came into full view.

It was a bus. A bus? Another bus wasn't supposed to pass by this way for several more hours! Then it dawned on me. Today was May Day, an important holiday in Marxist nations. Since people would be crowding the capital for government celebrations, extra buses had been scheduled to run all day. Sure enough, the bus stopped, took me on to the next mission hospital where I got a mechanic to return to the car with me. We resumed our journey soon afterward. The delay helped us avoid angry mobs in the capital city.

Is anything too hard for the Lord? Could He part the Red Sea for Israel? Could He bring a bus into the desert to rescue my family? Can He heal the emotions of guilt, discontent, or depression, and their physical consequences? The answer to all these questions is clear: Of course He can!

Has He Ever Left a Promise Unfulfilled? (Num.23:19)

By this point, I'm sure you've noticed that the eight years I spent in Ethiopia left a lasting impression on my life. If you'll bear with me a little longer, I'd like to share two more experiences that happened to me there.

The first is important in that it pertains to this question: Has God ever left a promise unfulfilled? Throughout Scripture, God has made certain promises which provide the basis for His prescriptions for health. For example, a promise we considered earlier—"If we confess our sins, He is faithful and just and will forgive us our sins" (1 John 1:9)—is a key to His remedy for guilt. Thus, it is important for us to acknowledge the truth and validity of all of God's promises if we are to experience healing.

That's where one of my experiences in Soddo comes into play. For some time, Christians in the region had strongly felt that God was leading them to construct a new hospital in southwest Ethiopia. The only problem was, the new facility would cost almost $250,000—and we didn't have nearly enough funds. Since we didn't have the necessary funds, that looked like a very expensive project.

But we remembered how God had promised the Israelites that if they rebuilt the temple *by faith,* He would be with them (Hag. 2:1-5). So, in faith, we decided to commence this project.

It would not be an exaggeration to say that our building program got off to an inauspicious start. Over a period of seven years, we went through four different builders. The first absconded with $72,000. Another told us he had to attend a wedding in Canada; he left after building two thirds of one floor and never returned. A third contractor had to resign for health reasons.

Finally, an Egyptian builder—who also was a Christian—signed a contract to take over the project, even though he knew we still needed to raise an additional $100,000 to cover construction costs. But he had caught our vision for this hospital and he believed that if God had promised to see this project through to completion—and we all believed He had—the necessary money would materialize.

Have you any doubts as to whether that hospital was completed? I'd hope not! God provided the funds we needed —as He promised He would—and the new hospital was busy before and after we left the country.

Has the Lord ever left a promise unfulfilled? Did He leave the temple unbuilt? Did Jesus renege on His promise to send His followers the Holy Spirit? (John 14:15-31) Are His promises to give us health-sustaining peace and contentment empty words? Never! The fact is, we can fully believe *all* of the Lord's promises—including those which apply to His prescriptions for health. Anyone who is truly interested in pursuing the quest for better physical and spiritual health must remember that fact.

Is the Lord's Arm Shortened That He Cannot Save? (Isa. 50:2)

My second "Ethiopian experience" relates to a rhetorical question that Isaiah once raised: Is God's arm too short that it cannot reach down and rescue us? (Isa. 50:2)

In recounting the story of our being marooned in the desert, I mentioned that we needed to "receive permission" to leave Ethiopia. This was due to the fact that after the *coup d'etat* of 1974, the government reserved the right to approve all foreigners' exit visas. That became a point of no small concern to my family and me.

After four years in Soddo, I had decided to return to the United States for further, advanced medical study. But the local citizens—who didn't want to lose the services of their resident surgeon—decided to block my way. Petitions were signed "requesting" that I stay in Ethiopia.

Just when it looked as though I might be spending the rest of my life as a guest of the government, the Ethiopian Minister of Health paid a visit to Soddo. Mustering my courage, I explained my ticklish predicament to him, hoping for his support. Fortunately, it turned out that he too was a physician, and he understood my desire to return to the States for further surgical training.

To make a long story short, the minister used his influence to help expedite our exit visas. On the aforementioned May Day, in a manner reminiscent of the escape scene from *The Sound of Music*, my family and I pushed our station wagon out to the road, drove past sleeping guards, and took our leave of this petulant African town.

Is God's arm too short to save? Hardly. I've no doubt that the Minister of Health was used of God to advance His will for my life. Thus, the minister didn't really help us escape Soddo; it was God's strong arm that delivered us.

The implications of this fact as they relate to our health are worth noting. No emotional or attitudinal problem, no physical disease, no infirmity of body or soul, is beyond His healing touch. Of that we can be sure.

Can God Spread a Table in the Desert? (Ps.78:19)

This is an important question for us to ponder. God did, in a manner of speaking, spread a feast for my family in the Ethiopian desert when our car broke down. He sent us a bus!

That experience testified to God's caring power, and clearly answered the psalmist's question. But the psalmist's query has an additional angle; he also is asking about God's *timing* in providing for us. When things seem hopeless, he wonders, when logic and circumstances argue against the fulfillment of His promises, can God still provide? Can He really spread a table in the desert?

During the most severe depression or the most fearful trial, we want to know if God really can provide for our deliverance. When our anger sends our digestive system into turmoil, we want to know if God really can provide healing.

When I hear these sorts of questions from my patients, I tell them a story I heard years ago of a young Chinese girl who grew up in a mission-run orphanage. For several months, this young orphan had been praying that she'd be able to give a gift to each of the other children in the orphanage at Christmas-time. What made her request so remarkable—apart from its utter selflessness—was that there were 186 other orphans in that particular institution!

As Christmas approached, the girl still had not received any money or gifts. But her faith in the Lord remained strong. Though she hadn't the faintest idea of how God was going to meet her request, her trust never waivered.

However, when Christmas Day finally arrived, it seemed as though her prayer had gone unanswered. She had no presents to give the other children. Heartbroken, she listlessly tugged at the ribbons of a gift the mission had secured for each child; she wondered why God hadn't heard her prayer.

Finally, she yanked off the ribbon and opened her box. *Wait! This couldn't be!* she thought. Peering into the box, nearly exploding with joy, she saw combs. Simple, unadorned hair combs—but there was one for every child in the orphanage! The young girl immediately sprang from her seat and happily began handing out her long-awaited gifts!

A member of the mission staff asked her what she was doing; the girl politely explained how God had answered her prayers and provided these combs. Someone contacted the church organization which had sent the gifts; the young orphan's story was confirmed. Apparently, one of the church workers had been in such a hurry to get all the children's gifts wrapped, she inadvertently put the combs together in one package—the very package God made certain reached that little girl.

From a human standpoint, this story seems absolutely preposterous. One hundred and eighty-six combs? Given to a little orphan girl? Ah, but our God is a God of miracles, and in faith, we can trust Him to provide for all our needs.

Can God spread a table in the desert? As surely as He can provide gifts to orphans and renewed health to those who love Him.

God's Prescriptions

It all seems too wonderful to be true, but God *does* care about our health, and He *has* provided the means by which we can improve it.

The key to this whole process is amazingly simple. We need only to recognize that a direct link exists between the health of our spirits and that of our bodies. And if our spirits are vibrant, strong, and growing, we stand a good chance of increasing the vitality of our bodies.

The Apostle John neatly summed up this truth when he stated:

> Dear friend, I pray that you may enjoy good health
> and that all may go well with you, even as your
> soul is getting along well (3 John 2).

May all our souls "get along well." And may the proof of that condition be evident in our bodies.

100533